No Pickle,
No Performance

NO PICKLE,
NO PERFORMANCE

An Irreverent Theatrical Excursion
from Tallulah to Travolta

HAROLD J. KENNEDY

Doubleday & Company, Inc.
Garden City, New York
1978

ISBN: 0-385-13241-7
Library of Congress Catalog Card Number 77–11767

Contents

[7]

Contents

Foreword

Sir James M. Barrie's Plain Jane heroine, Maggie Wylie, in *What Every Woman Knows* has a classic line where she says to her reluctant bridegroom, "I don't think anyone could love me who could not laugh at me a little."

Nothing could be more true in the wonderful crazy world of the theater. I have loved almost all of the more than a hundred major stars I have directed and appeared with during the past thirty-seven years, but I could never have loved them as much if I had not been able to laugh at them a little. There's a kind of basic insanity about our business that rubs off on everyone connected with it. Just as their avid fans often confuse the image with the reality, so do the stars themselves; and laughter is the only healthy antidote.

Moss Hart describes a roving band of actors in his valentine to show business, the delightful comedy *Light Up the Sky*, as follows:

> "*Mad, sire? Ah, yes—mad indeed,*
> *But observe how they do*
> *light up the sky.*"

And he ascribes the quote to Old Skroob from a play called *The Idle Jeste*.

But Moss also walked a thin line between illusion and reality. It turned out after *Light Up the Sky* opened and people were curious about the quote that there was no such character as Old Skroob and no such play as *The Idle Jeste*. Moss made it up to suit the needs of his own play.

Imaginary or real? In our business what's the difference? There's always only a thin line between.

This is meant to be an affectionate book. It is also meant to be an amusing book. And I can only hope that if you laugh at these people with me you will grow to love them as I have.

H.J.K.

No Pickle,
No Performance

NO PICKLE,
NO PERFORMANCE

This book is dedicated to the lady whose challenge provided its title. Her name is Renee Taylor and she is a writer of some wit and an actress whose talent, perhaps, was better suited to performing her own material. Her ego is formidable even in a business of monumental ones. I know something about actors' egos since in my thirty-seven years in the professional theater I have directed and appeared in more than three hundred plays with a wide variety of stars including Orson Welles, Helen Hayes, Gloria Swanson, Tallulah Bankhead, Jane Cowl, Miriam Hopkins, Ginger Rogers, Charlton Heston, Luise Rainer, Robert Ryan, Steve Allen, and Jayne Meadows and only two summers ago John Travolta, the new sex symbol of the younger generation. It is a far cry from Ina Claire to John Travolta and there are many amusing tales along the way. This book will attempt to relate some of them.

But back to Renee Taylor. Miss Taylor was to play the role of the shoplifter in my planned Broadway revival of Sidney

Kingsley's play *Detective Story*. It was the role that made a star out of Lee Grant in the original production and is generally regarded as being one of the show-stealing parts in contemporary theater. Miss Taylor had originally wanted to play the role of the wife but Lee Strasberg told her the shoplifter was a better part so she switched to that.

It is a warm, touching, sad, and rather pathetic part, but very funny, and as it turned out Miss Taylor really wanted none of those things. In the few performances she finally did perform at Paramus, New Jersey, where we tried out the play, she brought her own hairdresser from New York who spent an hour and a half every night making her up as though she were going to play Salome and do the dance of the Seven Veils.

In rehearsal she constantly made us change lines that were the very essence of the character. Because of her loneliness and inability to get a man, this pathetic little lady has been driven into a minor case of shoplifting. An alligator bag. Imitation alligator, as she sadly explains. And she has a speech where she explains her plight to a sympathetic detective:

"Get married? Get me a man, I'll marry him. Anything. As long as it's got pants. You think I'd be here? A rotten crocodile bag. I'd be home cooking him such a meal. Get married, it's easy to talk."

Miss Taylor refused to say a single line of that speech. "There isn't an audience in the world," she explained modestly, "that would believe I couldn't get any man I wanted."

The shoplifter also had a long scene on the telephone with her brother-in-law pleading with him to come down and bail her out. When she finally succeeds and he promises to come, she hangs up the phone, relieved, and says:

"Yeah. All I can do is thank God my sister's sexy."

Miss Taylor insisted on changing the line to:

"Thank God my sister's sexy too," and defeated the whole point.

The end came when she appeared at rehearsal one day with half a dozen typewritten sheets of additional dialogue which she had written for herself and had decided to put into the play. Out of morbid curiosity I took a look at the pages. They were a lot of jokes, not bad jokes, but having no relationship to that scene.

There are some arguments a director doesn't have to get into. There are too many other people who will quickly pick up the cudgels for him. I explained to Miss Taylor that there was such a thing as the Dramatists' Guild and that there was also a very much living author named Sidney Kingsley. If Miss Taylor wanted to indulge in a battle of egos, formidable though she was, I'd put my money on Sidney Kingsley any day.

"I'll call the author and see what he says," I told Renee. I called Sidney and he said exactly what I knew he'd say.

"Get her out of the show." Period. End of discussion.

It was easy to get her out of the show because she had already told me she would walk out unless she was allowed to insert the extra lines, so it was mutually agreed that she would play the two tryout weeks at Paramus, which was a stock engagement, and be replaced for the Philadelphia and the hoped-for Broadway run.

We continued with rehearsals and the play opened a series of three previews in Paramus on a Friday night as scheduled. The first act went extremely well but shortly after the second act started, Miss Taylor began going over to the other actors and confronting them with all the lines that had been on those rejected pages. The actors, of course, had never heard any of them before and obviously on an opening night were completely thrown by them. They reacted in two ways, both disastrous to the play. The inexperienced actors became so nervous that they fluffed their own lines; the experienced ones were so enraged that they snarled their lines at her in such a way that all the sympathetic characters began to behave like heavies. It looked as though all those seemingly nice detectives were going to beat up this poor little shoplifter, which several of them seriously considered doing.

When the second act curtain finally came down, I sent for the Equity deputy.

"Go to her dressing room," I said, "and tell that woman that

if she says one line in the third act that is not in the script I
will have the stage manager ring down the curtain and I will go
out in front of it and explain why we have done it."

Needless to say, the third act went off without incident but
the company was in turmoil and there were threats of bringing
her up on charges at Equity and even more violent suggestions
from some of the more volatile members of the cast.

Any crisis in the theater always occurs on a Friday night. Equity is closed for the weekend; every agent has taken off to his
country manse; and there is never anything that can be done
about a Friday night crisis until Monday morning.

We had two performances back to back the next night, Saturday, and they both went extremely well with no nonsense
from Miss Taylor. So I decided, ill-advisedly, that it was fortunate we had done nothing further about her.

Sunday was the official opening night with the critics out
front. At exactly half hour the stage manager, Bruce Blaine,
came to my dressing room and said, "Mr. Kennedy, we have a
problem."

"Oh, God," I said, "what?"

"There is no pickle with Miss Taylor's sandwich."

"There isn't supposed to be a pickle with Miss Taylor's
sandwich," I said.

"I know that," he said. "And the prop man knows it. But
completely by accident there was a pickle with each of the
sandwiches during the three previews. And now she says she
won't do the play without one."

"That's ridiculous," I said.

"I know that."

"You go and talk to her."

"I already have."

"What did she say?"

"She said, 'No pickle, no performance.' "

I have a practice which has worked well over the years that
no matter how outrageously someone behaves on an opening
night before the curtain goes up you do everything possible to

keep peace and quiet backstage. Opening night nerves are bad enough for everyone involved without extraneous irritations.

"Get her the damn pickle," I said.

"We can't."

And then he explained to me how the whole situation had evolved. The Bergen Mall, where the Playhouse is located, is a bustling place all week long but on Sunday it is like a sealed-up convent. Even the hot dog stand in the bowling alley isn't open. Miss Taylor's sandwiches for the previews had been bought at the coffee shop across the street which, of course, was closed on Sundays. Knowing this the prop man had stopped on his way to work at a restaurant some distance away and bought all the food required for the opening night performance. Wherever he stopped obviously didn't provide pickles with their sandwiches, and since there was nothing in the play that remotely suggested the necessity of a pickle he hadn't noticed or cared that there wasn't one.

"Tell him to go anywhere," I said, "and find a pickle. Even if we have to hold the curtain."

"He doesn't want to," Bruce said. "He's furious."

I was furious too, but in the theater nothing matters on an opening night but getting that play on that stage. "Send him to me," I said.

The prop man fortunately was a lovely man and that rare breed of stagehand who really cares about the theater. I had done five other productions at Paramus and he had been most cooperative with all of them and had also been a great admirer of my Broadway revival of *The Front Page*, which originated at Paramus. He was genuinely outraged at Miss Taylor and didn't want to do anything for her. I explained to him that if he would indeed somehow try to find a pickle he would not be doing her a favor but in fact a special favor to me and to the entire production. He finally somewhat reluctantly agreed and got into his car and went off in search of the holy pickle.

When fifteen minutes was called by Mr. Blaine, it was obviously too early to have heard from him. When five minutes was called I was hopeful. But no word. When it came time for places to be called he still had not returned.

"We're holding," Mr. Blaine told the company when it was time for the curtain to go up.

In the theater when you say that you are "holding" it is usually because there is a line at the box office or people are straggling in late and you want to get the whole audience seated before the play starts. Only Mr. Blaine and Miss Taylor and myself knew what "we're holding" meant that night.

Seven minutes after the advertised curtain Mr. Blaine came happily to my dressing room door.

"The pickle is on the stage. Places, please, Mr. Kennedy."

The play went better that night than it had ever gone but I must say I couldn't wait for that third act curtain to come down. I went back to my dressing room exhausted and irritated. When Mr. Blaine came to my door I told him to be sure to send the prop man to me so I could thank him.

"Oh, he's perfectly happy," said Mr. Blaine.

"He is?" I asked, somewhat surprised.

"Yes. They had a little ceremony before the show—you'd be surprised what they did to the pickle."

Gloria Swanson had a wonderful reaction when I told her this story.

"Poor Miss Taylor," Gloria said. "Can't you see her shopping around to every delicatessen in New York complaining that she can never find a pickle here to match the caliber of that one she had in New Jersey."

The evening was wrapped up by the head stagehand who called into my dressing room as he was leaving the theater:

"Well, we gave her the pickle; where the hell was the performance?"

The *Bergen County Record*, the most important paper in the area, gave the opening night performance of *Detective Story* a rave review: "With a play like this and stars of this caliber, and a director like Mr. Kennedy, one's hopes are so high that you feel you must be doomed to eventual disappointment, but seeing the production of *Detective Story* on Sunday night was like opening your new mink coat for Christmas and finding it lined in cloth of gold."

But unlike my revival of *The Front Page*, after which it was patterned and which bore the kiss of success from the first day of rehearsal, *Detective Story* suffered from the beginning from a firmly implanted kiss of death.

Our original cast for the production, on the basis of which we got our bookings at the Shubert in Philadelphia and the Helen Hayes Theatre in New York and raised all of the money, included Barry Nelson, Renee Taylor, Dina Merrill, Robert Alda, Tom Ewell, Walter Abel, Peggy Wood, Rita Gam, Russell Nype, and Marty Brill. All above the title. By the time we got to Philadelphia we were lucky we still had the title. And when Sidney Kingsley got through with us we didn't even have that.

Peggy Wood's husband died the first day of rehearsal and she quite understandably withdrew from the show. Miss Taylor went by mutual agreement. Sidney Kingsley, who had agreed to exercise approval only of the principal male starring role, reneged and made us get rid of Dina Merrill, Robert Alda, Walter Abel, and Russell Nype, all of whom contributed, he said, to making it look like a "geriatric" revival of his play. With all the other casting problems the management delayed getting Tom Ewell his contract and he took another job. Neither the producers nor Sidney liked what they called Barry Nelson's "cerebral" performance, but I stood firm on that one and Barry was with us to the end. The juvenile's wife's mother had a heart attack in California and his wife, who was also his manager, took him out of the play overnight in Paramus. The lady friend and manager of another actor, who was apparently a little AC-DC, removed him from the show because there were too many men in it. And then, of course, there was Rita Gam.

Rita Gam is an absolutely enchanting lady who, I have always felt, must have been born just this side of the dark of the moon. I have never understood any conversation I have ever had with her, but I was fascinated by her, and she too was with us to the end.

With a cast of thirty-four people I was allowed only one dress rehearsal on the set and that was in Paramus on the afternoon of the first public preview. Because of Equity's rule about a dinner break for the actors, by the time the rehearsal was over I had only forty-two minutes to give all my notes on the production. And since it was the first time on the set, I had countless ones. I was racing through them as fast as I could and the entire cast was sitting on the stage furniture and cross-legged on the stage floor, dutifully absorbing them.

In the middle of the notes, Rita Gam raised her hand.

"I have a question."

"Is it important?" I said. "I have very little time."

"It's very important."

"I hope so."

"In the event of fire," Rita said, "do you want us to continue with the play or return to our dressing rooms?"

I have told this story to people in the theater and they all insist I have made it up, but fortunately I have thirty-four witnesses to it.

Another day, after the opening in Philadelphia, the whole cast was grouped on the stage in much the same way and I was standing in the orchestra pit, leaning on the stage and giving notes.

"I can't hear you," called out a voice from the second balcony.

I looked up and there was a figure huddled in the very last row.

"Who is that?" I asked.

"It's Miss Gam," said the voice.

"What the hell are you doing up there?" I bellowed.

"Oh, good," she said, "I can hear you now."

And on the closing day in Philadelphia she called Bruce Blaine in his hotel room at five minutes after nine in the morning and said:

"Mr. Blaine, this is Miss Gam. I've just had an obscene phone call."

Bruce looked at the clock. He had two shows to do and a production to close down. "I'm sorry, Miss Gam," he said, "but I don't know what I can do about it."

"You can come down and move me out of this hotel."

"I'm afraid I can't do that. Anyway, there isn't much point in moving. We're closing today and going back to New York tonight."

"I can't stay in a hotel where I get obscene phone calls," Rita said.

"What did they say, Miss Gam?" Bruce asked.

"They said, 'Miss Gam, you're a ham.' "

So *Detective Story*, for which I had such high hopes, closed as it had begun on kind of a crazy note. Barry Nelson and I drove sadly back to New York together, remembering that mink coat and the cloth of gold. We still think it could have worked.

ORSON WELLES

ORSON WELLES GAVE ME my first job in the theater.

When I came to New York, by way of Dartmouth College and the Yale School of Drama, Orson was the hottest thing on Broadway. He had not yet received the national recognition which came to him, whether he liked it or not, from his world-shaking broadcast about the Martians, *The War of the Worlds*. By that time I was working with him.

But in 1938 his modern dress production of *Julius Caesar* was packing them in at the tiny Mercury Theatre on West Forty-first Street near Sixth Avenue and people like Katharine Cornell felt privileged to get standing room at the special midnight performances on Saturday nights for the benefit of the acting profession. *Julius Caesar* was being played in repertory with three other productions. *The Shoemaker's Holiday, Danton's Death,* and *Heartbreak House;* and the acting company included Orson, who had all the best parts, and Joseph Cotten, Arlene Francis, Martin Gabel, Vincent Price, Edith Barrett,

Mady Christians, Paul Stewart, and Everett Sloane. An impressive group. And all working for minimum. As I found out years later with both *The Front Page* and *Detective Story*, which were presented under much the same circumstances, when you have people of that caliber and a first-rate project no real actor cares about the money. There wasn't an actor in town who wouldn't have been happy to be a part of Orson's Mercury Theatre.

So when he announced that he was going to send out a road company of *Julius Caesar* and issued an open call for the bit parts and the modern-day equivalent of the spear carriers, every actor in town did indeed show up. I got to Forty-first Street an hour and a half before the call and found not only the theater itself overflowing but the alley beside it and the street in front of it. It was an impossible mob scene and I gave up and went home. I went back to the theater that night and was able to buy a single standing-room ticket for the performance. And with the courage that they breed at Yale Drama School I waited in the alley for Orson afterward.

"Mr. Welles," I said when he came out the stage door.

"Yes," said Orson in that voice that sounded exactly like the Hammond organ he had used so brilliantly throughout the show.

"I was here to see you today."

"Well, obviously I can't see everybody," Orson said.

"I know," I said, "and since you are only looking for bit parts I would think it would be awfully difficult to choose among all those people."

"It is."

"What if I gave you a reason why I would be better than any of the others?" I asked.

"What could such a reason be?"

"Well, it would be money in your pocket," I said.

"That," said Orson, "would constitute a very substantial reason. Come. We will have a drink."

We went to a slightly sleazy bar at the corner of Broadway

and Forty-first Street and I explained to Orson the idea that I had worked out during the day. All day at home I had brooded, trying to figure out what I might have that none of those hundreds of other actors had that might land me one of those tiny parts. All I really had were two college degrees and that has nothing to do with acting. It might, however, have something to do with something else.

So I came up with the plan that I outlined to Orson. On my own time and at my own expense I would book myself as a free lecturer on Shakespeare at every high school, college, and private school in the various cities on the schedule. I would do the play at night and get up every morning for early assemblies, luncheon speeches, afternoon seminars, whatever. I would, by a strange coincidence, talk mostly about Orson's production of *Julius Caesar*. I could truthfully say I thought it was brilliant, and I could quite subtly peddle blocks of tickets to the production.

"Do you think the schools would take you?" asked Orson.

"They're always looking for free speakers," I said. "And I think with my academic credits plus the prestige of being a member of your company, they would grab me."

"It's a brilliant idea," said Orson. "You're hired. And you will play Statilius."

"Who is Statilius?" I asked.

"I don't know," said Orson, "but there is a line in the play—'Statilius showed the light and was seen no more'—it's a perfect part for you.

I did indeed play Statilius, opening at the National Theatre in Washington, D.C. And for the first two weeks I showed the light; and after that I was mostly seen no more.

It is dangerous in the theater to be too good at your job, particularly if that job is not the job you want to do. Actors are a dime a dozen. A good stage manager, a crackerjack press agent, or, as in my case, a ticket-selling lecturer, is far more valuable to any management.

By the end of the second week of the tour, well over one third of the tickets being sold at the box office were in huge blocks of seats purchased by the various schools and colleges where I had lectured. I was promptly taken out of the play and sent one week ahead to lecture and build up the advance sales.

From then on I appeared only on opening night in each town when the company caught up with me, rather like a guest soloist at the ballet. These opening nights were also embarrassing, as they would be filled with large groups of loyal students who had heard me speak at their schools the preceding week and who would accord me an enormous ovation on my first appearance. Needless to say, this was somewhat annoying to the actors playing Brutus and Cassius and Mark Antony, who got no recognition on their first appearances. But there was nothing they could do about it. Statilius was the star of the road company on Monday nights.

This unexpected and tumultuous reception accorded me caused considerable confusion in the company the first time it occurred. All the supporting actors came racing out of their dressing rooms and rushed onto the stage thinking it was the first act curtain.

Orson was the most brilliant director I have ever worked with. His staging of the opening scene of *Julius Caesar* was absolutely inspired and I never tired of watching it. It wasn't the opening scene of the play as Shakespeare had written it. Orson shrewdly started the play much further into the script, eliminating all the endless fanfare and tedious exposition from the actual opening scenes of the play. In Orson's version, the house lights dimmed slowly. Then the theater was plunged in total blackness. There was one loud discordant peal on the organ. And a weird voice called out from the back of the theater, usually from the projection booth, "Caesar. Ceeeeesar. CAESAR." Then every light on the stage plunged up full. There was Caesar standing in front of his legions. He would stride directly to the front of the stage and call out into the darkened auditorium, "Who is there in the crowd that calls on me? Set him before me; let me see his face." An electrifying beginning for an electrifying show.

As an actor, however, Orson has always been an enigma to me. He will sit in a bar and give the most hilarious impersonations of what he considered "ham" actors, like John Barrymore in the declining years and John Carradine. But when he played the same kind of roles himself, as in *Jane Eyre* on the screen, he gave a factual, almost exact duplication of the very performances he had so devastatingly lampooned. You might indeed just as well be watching John Carradine.

I had returned from the road and was working with Orson in New York when he did *The War of the Worlds*. The question I was most often asked about the Martian broadcast in subsequent lectures was this:

"Didn't Orson Welles do it deliberately as a publicity stunt?"

The answer is simple. He didn't. He would have if he had thought of it; he just never thought of it.

As a matter of fact, I distinctly recall that at the first run-through of the radio show we thought *The War of the Worlds* was pretty dull and I remember Orson exhorting the actors to work harder and try to put a little pace and life and excitement into the script. Apparently we had a fair degree of success.

Nothing that has been written about the Martian broadcast has been exaggerated. It did indeed create a national panic. The switchboards at CBS have never since been so deluged with frantic calls. People were genuinely terrified. I used to tell funny stories about the reactions to the broadcast on my subsequent lecture tours but I stopped telling them because people didn't appreciate them. I told what I thought were some hilarious anecdotes about the broadcast at a girls' school in Washington, D.C., and didn't get a single laugh. I found out after the lecture that the headmistress of the school had heard the broadcast and locked all of the girls in the chapel where they spent the whole night on their knees in community prayer.

My own feeling about the broadcast was that if you had

heard it from the beginning and all the way through it couldn't possibly have frightened anyone. But I think it was a question of "dialitis." Orson was on the air opposite Charlie McCarthy, who was then at the peak of his popularity, and I think it is safe to assume that most people were listening to Charlie. During a commercial on Charlie's show or when a dead air guest like Nelson Eddy came on, the audience may have switched their dials and caught a few words of our program, probably the simulated news flashes.

I always liked Alexander Woollcott's dismissal of the whole affair. "I have always maintained," Woollcott wrote, "that the intelligent people listened to Charlie McCarthy."

I did quite a bit of lecturing for Orson around New York and soon became his social alter ego. I would be sent in his place to all the functions he didn't want to attend and eat his chicken à la king and speak in his behalf and accept awards and bestow plaques. I also arranged several high-paying lecture dates around the country for Orson himself.

My fondest recollection of these was a lecture he gave in a large western city. It was either Denver or Omaha. I'm quite sure it was Omaha. But in any case, the day of the lecture there was a terrific blizzard and only about forty-six people showed up in a three-thousand-seat auditorium.

The chairlady, a typical one, got up breezy and undaunted, and introduced Orson.

"Mr. Welles," she said, "is an actor, an author, a director, a producer, and a lecturer."

"There are so many of me," said Orson, as he took his bow. "And so few of you."

I reluctantly left Orson and the Mercury Theatre. First, because I was aware that I was too valuable to them in all the wrong areas ever to get the chance to act and direct, which is what I wanted to do.

And second, because when I gave a lecture at Columbia University, pinch-hitting for Orson, a lecture bureau agent named Harold R. Peat came backstage afterward and said to me:

"Don't ever open your mouth for nothing again. You can get a lot of money for doing what you're doing."

So for the next couple of years he sent me out on the Town Hall lecture series and I spoke twice at Town Hall in New York, three times each in Buffalo and Cleveland, and five times in Detroit, and in many other places. I did indeed make a lot of money. But it wasn't what I wanted. So in 1940 I opened my own summer theater at the Kirby Memorial Theatre on the campus of Amherst College where I presented a season I am still proud of with some of the biggest names of the day, including Jane Cowl, Ina Claire, Tallulah Bankhead, Ruth Chatterton, Edward Everett Horton, Sylvia Sidney, and Luther Adler, and Thornton Wilder starring in his own play, *Our Town*.

In all the years since I have never seen Orson Welles again.

JANE COWL
AND THE ARABS

Jane Cowl played for me that first season at Amherst. She was supposed to do S. N. Behrman's *No Time for Comedy* but she called me casually one day and announced that she had switched to Bernard Shaw's *Captain Brassbound's Conversion*. That's quite a switch. Behrman's play has eight actors and two simple sets. Shaw's play has twenty-five major speaking parts, three gigantic sets, and, on top of all this, two rival bands of Arabs who come swarming on the stage at the end of the second act. It was a little like being asked to produce a full-scale opera when you were planning an evening of lantern slides.

We had to up the budget and we hired all the additional speaking parts from New York but obviously in summer stock it was impractical to import two rival bands of Arabs. I looked around to see what I could do locally. As luck seemed to have it, the Amherst College football team was in pre-season training. We worked it out with the college to have the boys be football players by day and marauding Arabs at night. They were a husky group and very enthusiastic and the wardrobe woman sewed some bedsheets together for them for costumes. They brought their own jock straps from the gym and it looked for a time as though we had indeed been blessed.

Most of the Arabs had nothing to do but groan and grunt and shake their spears at each other but there were two speaking parts: the Sidi, who was the chief of one band, and the Cadi, who was the head of the other. For these roles we chose the two hunkiest and chunkiest of the lot who turned out to be the quarterback and the fullback of the team. I rehearsed them extensively, especially the Cadi, who had to leer at Jane at the end of the act, and snarl: "I am taking you to the mountains," or something to that effect.

Then he had to throw her over his shoulder and carry her off. Curtain.

When we got to the dress rehearsal and Jane was with us for the first time the minor Arabs were marvelous. They grunted and groaned and threatened Jane as though they had been with Stella Adler all their lives. But the two boys who had the lines were extremely nervous and their voices rose an octave or two, especially the one who had the line, "I am taking you to the mountains." He did indeed sound like the child Freddie Bartholomew in *Little Lord Fauntleroy*. But of course no twenty-year-old boy anywhere had a voice as deep as Jane's.

Jane immediately decided they were both pansies. A quaint word popular in the forties.

"They're football players," I told her.

"Football players are the worst," Jane said. "And no pansy is going to take me to the mountains."

After considerable discussion she finally agreed that the Sidi could stay but the Cadi had to go and someone else would have to carry her off to the mountains. On a quiet Sunday night in Amherst, Massachusetts, in the middle of August I had no idea who that ballsy someone was going to be.

I called Smith College in the neighboring town of Northampton and asked whether any of the faculty, who might still be in summer residence, ever did any acting. It seemed that they did, and it seemed even more remarkable that the faculty had done a production of *Captain Brassbound's Conversion* that very spring and were looking forward to seeing ours. They put me in touch with the professor in charge and I couldn't believe our good fortune when it turned out that he himself had played the Cadi in the college production. He was interested and available and would be thrilled to walk on the stage with Jane Cowl.

I was too young then to realize what I have since learned in the theater. Beware when luck seems to be smiling too benignly upon you.

He drove over for rehearsal the next morning and he was handsome and muscular and virile beyond any possible doubt. He had the added advantage of having a wife and two children, whom he brought with him, and we thought that would reassure Jane. It wouldn't reassure anyone today, but those were innocent times. In any case, Jane cringed with delighted terror when he snarled at her, "I am taking you to the mountains."

That night I went to the opening performance and took his wife as my guest. She was extremely nervous during the entire first act.

"I don't know why you're so nervous," I told her at intermission. "Your husband was marvelous at rehearsal."

"He always is," she said. "At rehearsal."

There was something about her reading of those last two words that made me more nervous than she was.

"What do you mean by that?" I asked.

"Well, he gets very nervous in a performance," she said. "And he—well, he stutters."

"Stutters?" I said.

"Well, not exactly stutters," she said. "It's just really that no words come out at all."

I returned to my seat and sat through the second act like a frozen robin. Finally at the end of the act there came the offstage roar of the adolescent Arabs. Onto the stage they stomped, led by the Sidi on the one hand and the Cadi on the other. The Cadi was a magnificent figure and had the best-looking bedsheet of the lot. He advanced upon Jane in a totally menacing manner. There was hope. Then he opened his mouth.

His wife was right. He didn't stutter. Not at all. Just, simply, not a word came out. His lips quivered and his bedsheet shook like a big tent in a sandstorm. Still not a single syllable came out.

Jane waited as long as she could. Finally she looked directly at him.

"Do you want to take me to the mountains?" she said.

He nodded his head in dumb assent.

"Let's go," said Jane and she swept off the stage dragging him by the hand behind her.

It was a terrific second-act curtain but made for some confusion in the third act where Jane was supposed to be an unwilling captive.

Twelve years later I wrote this story as a segment for the popular "Mama" series with Peggy Wood. I played myself, while Dick Van Patten, as Nels, played the original college boy who in the script didn't get replaced but, as the Cadi, encountered all of the same problems. It was one of their most popular shows.

THORNTON WILDER

ONE OF THE GREAT JOYS of the season at Amherst was having
Thornton Wilder play the stage manager for me in his own
lovely play, *Our Town*. To me it has always been the definitive
American play and though Thornton was certainly no actor he
was the definitive casting for the small town commentator on
the play. There was something extra special in having the author speak his own words to you and with Thornton's New
England accent and his slightly old maid manner, the words really came to life through the lips of the man who wrote them.
When he said at the end of the first act, "You can go out and
smoke now—those that smoke," you sensed the implicit small
town disapproval of the act.

Thornton asked for one day off from rehearsals to go to New
York and see *Hellzapoppin* and I thought that was an odd
thing for him to be so eager to see. But when he came back he
invited me for cocktails and said with great excitement, "I have
just found my new play. I am going to write the story of man's
survival in a *Hellzapoppin* technique." And that was the origin
of *The Skin of Our Teeth*.

[33]

A GOOSE FOR
GLORIA SWANSON

I WROTE MY first Broadway play because Gloria Swanson locked me in a hotel room and made me write it.

We have done seventeen separate productions together over the past thirty-seven years, two of them plays I wrote especially for her: one, *A Goose for the Gander*, which got to Broadway; and the other, the one that should have gotten there, in its various incarnations called *The Inkwell*, *Just for Tonight*, and finally *Reprise*.

Gloria is a perfectionist, which is marvelous for a director but can be a pain in the ass to ordinary mortals who have long since made their peace with mediocrity. Gloria stoutly believes that people are basically stupid and she wages a fierce and unending battle against ineptitude. She has no patience with minor nuisances like standing in line, social security numbers, long distance phone operators, or the American Medical Association. She can never hold on to a cook for the simple reason that anything the cook can cook Gloria can cook better. She has never kept a maid for more than five days because Gloria can and does get down on her hands and knees and clean the floor better.

She is impossible with scene designers, prop people, and lighting technicians. Impossible from their point of view because she knows exactly what she wants and will settle for nothing less. She will take the trouble to show a reluctant electrician the difference in her appearance when she is lighted straight on from the balcony rail, or crosslighted, or lighted from underneath by those magical footlights which all those ladies love, as against the harsh and aging effect of overhead light. Unlike most stars of a certain age who insist on specific colors, usually pink, Gloria isn't interested in the color of the lights, she is interested only in the source of the light.

When she sends the scenic designer explicit instructions that the mantel on the fireplace is to be four feet six and a quarter inches high, that is what she means. And it better not be six and one eighth. She will know in a second and if there is any discussion she'll bring her tape measure out on the stage with her. None of this is quite as cavalier as it may sound; there is good reason for it. She is a meticulous actress and she knows how to posture herself well and effectively. If she plans to lean an elbow on the mantel she wants it to be at the exact angle that is flattering and becoming. Nor does she want to fall off balance and hit her chin when she discovers that what she is leaning on is substantially lower than she thought it was.

She is, however, generous and gracious and completely cooperative with fellow actors and she has always been wonderful to me in our actor-director relationship. I think in the theater we tend to remember and deal with people always in the terms on which we first met them. If an actress or director first meets you as an apprentice in stock, or an office boy, you will pretty much always remain that person to them. In the same way, all of us who idolized the great stars of the past always remember them that way regardless of what lows they may, sadly, sink to.

When Gloria met me and I directed her first play I knew a

great deal more about the theater than she did. In her mind, I think, it has always stayed that way. In thirty-five years she has never challenged me on a piece of direction, and I doubt if she ever will. She seems, as in the beginning, always eager for my approval.

I went to see her on Broadway when she went into the cast of *Butterflies Are Free*. It was the first time I had ever seen her on a stage because all the rest of the times I had been up there with her. She had insisted I come, and had left me a special seat in the fifth row center on the aisle.

I found the play very touching and Gloria quite lovely in it. I am a great audience so I cried all through the second act. When the final curtain fell I went down to the men's room in the lobby to bathe my eyes, so I was a little late getting backstage.

When I got there Gloria was standing outside the stage door in full costume and makeup, looking frantically up and down Shubert Alley.

"I thought you hadn't liked me," she said.

If Gloria should decide to telephone you after not having seen you for six years she would be irritated beyond belief if you were not instantly on the other end of the phone to receive her call. It is a perfectly natural reaction; if she wants to talk to you, she assumes you should be there.

When I was most deeply involved in productions with her she made the automatic assumption that if I were not at home I had to be at Sardi's. I usually was, but not always. If Gloria got no answer at the hotel, she would phone Sardi's, ask the maître d' if I were there, and if he said no, demand to speak to Vincent Sardi.

"Is Mr. Kennedy not there?"

"No, Miss Swanson," Vincent would say.

"Have you looked at the bar?"

"Yes, Miss Swanson."

"He's not at home; he must be there."

"He isn't, Miss Swanson."

"Well, where is he?"

"I don't know, Miss Swanson."

"Well, find him."

These ladies lead very rarefied lives and are not prepared to deal with the minor nuisances we mortals have to cope with. (Lynn Fontanne, entering the Shubert Theatre one night, was genuinely surprised to be asked for her tickets. "Tickets are for other people," she said.) The most endearing thing about Gloria is that she does have a sense of humor about all this, but only after you point it out to her. She will roar with laughter when I imitate her doing the inquisition of Vincent Sardi, and in the midst of the laughter she will say: "Oh, I never did that; you're making it all up."

We first met in 1942 when I read in the Sunday *Times* that she was thinking of doing a Broadway play. I wrote her and suggested that if she were thinking of trying Broadway, since she had never been on a stage in her life, she better get her feet wet in summer stock first.

"Find out whether you like the stage," I wrote her. "And whether it likes you."

I got an immediate response from her and went to her apartment at Fifth Avenue and Seventy-third Street where she still lives.

"What do you mean whether it likes me?" she asked.

"It might not," I said.

"Then we damn well better find out."

I took her a dozen scripts and she chose George Kelly's play *Reflected Glory*, which Tallulah had done on Broadway. It wasn't a very good play but it was a good vehicle for Gloria as it allowed her to be flamboyant and to wear a number of dazzling gowns which, of course, is exactly what her audience wanted.

We opened on a split week, four days in a high school auditorium in Poughkeepsie, with Eleanor Roosevelt attending the opening, and the final two days at the summer theater in Pawling, New York, where the final performance was enlivened by the appearance of the local sheriff who lugged the management off to jail for nonpayment of my director's fee.

Before that first performance in Poughkeepsie Gloria told me frankly that she had no idea what I might be entitled to expect. She had not only never been on a stage before; she had literally never opened her mouth in public even at a premiere or a benefit. She had always been too frightened to do it. Now she was having nightmares all week that she would get out there, open her mouth, and nothing would come out.

"If that happens," she said, "and it may, just bring down the curtain and give them their money back. I can always go back to silent pictures."

It was agreed that I was to hold the script, sitting crosslegged in the fireplace all during the play except for the one brief scene that I was in. On opening night when places were called I took my position there and Gloria took hers offstage on the opposite side of the stage.

When the curtain went up the pages of the script were rattling so in my hands that I was sure the people in the first row could hear them. On the other side of the stage poor Gloria's heart was beating like the drums in *The Emperor Jones*. She told me afterward that her heart was pounding so hard she really thought she was going to die right on the spot. And when her entrance cue came she didn't care if she did.

But the minute she walked on the stage, she said, and even before she said her first line, the most extraordinary calm came over her.

"But I've always been here," she said to herself. "This is where I belong."

She knew that when she opened her mouth all of the words were going to come out. Indeed they did. She didn't miss a syllable throughout the entire performance; but, as a matter of fact, her nerves had made the other actors so nervous that she had to prompt the rest of the company several times.

We had a very successful ten-week tour. Business was very brisk and the matinees set new house records everywhere. It isn't true that romantic male stars are the big matinee draws in summer stock. It is the ladies like Gloria and Tallulah and Arlene Francis and Kitty Carlisle who pack them in at the matinees. Women feel they know these ladies intimately; they want to see what they look like in person; what they're wearing; what their hairdos are like; and how old they really look. They discuss all of this audibly during the performance. Those were the days of the old fifty-cent matinees on the New York City subway circuit at the Flatbush in Brooklyn and the Windsor in the Bronx. We had to play four matinees a week: Wednesday, Thursday, Saturday, and Sunday. When Gloria played the subway circuit that summer all four matinees were sold out way beyond capacity, with housewives sitting in the aisles, on the stairways, and standing five deep in the back. Not a man in the house.

When we went back there the second summer in Rachel Crothers' *Let Us Be Gay*, in which I was playing a much bigger part at Gloria's insistence, I was on stage when Gloria made her first entrance and we had an intimate ten-minute scene together on the couch.

It was literally impossible to hear each other's cues. The ladies in the audience talked to each other at full voice, about Gloria's age—she was forty-three at the time and they already thought she was seventy—about her clothes, and, of course, about her husbands.

At a Thursday matinee at the Flatbush in Brooklyn we heard one lady say loud and clear above the others:

"Well, Gilbert Roland was one."

Gloria got up from the couch and walked right down to the footlights.

"Well, he wasn't," she said.

Gloria has always been very patient about references, however inaccurate, to her age. She did indeed start so young at the old Essanay Studios in Chicago and she had been a star for so long in silent films and such a legend so early that it was understandable people should think she was a great deal older than she actually was. The only times she got angry at any implication of age, and she used to get apoplectic, were when she would make a casual reference to her mother who died just a few years ago.

"Your MOTHER???" people would exclaim in disbelief, as though her mother must have been well buried for a hundred years.

Let Us Be Gay was a much better play for us than Reflected Glory and we played it for the next couple of summers with great success everywhere. It is a tribute to our mutual innocence that we did the play for four years without ever realizing that the title had any implications other than what Miss Crothers meant, which was Let Us Be Lively. I suppose if we were to revive it today we would have to change the title: the raciest thing in it is the fact that Gloria plays a divorcee—pretty racy at the time the play was written but perhaps a severe disappointment, with that title, to today's audiences.

We took Let Us Be Gay to the Hanna Theatre in Cleveland in 1943 when they were having a season of summer stock. For economy's sake I had combined the three sets the play called for into one set, the outdoor patio of a Long Island home with a balcony upstage. The balcony had been a separate set in the original play and the whole second act was played on it.

We were playing the old Erlanger Theatre in Buffalo the week before and we invited the Cleveland designer and his technical staff over to Buffalo to see the physical production there so they could duplicate it exactly and avoid any last-minute problems. They came and made careful notes, but when we arrived in Cleveland we had nothing but problems.

The designer gave us quite a lovely set but although he had seen the show and knew the whole second act was played on the balcony he had covered the entire balcony with a gorgeous heavy latticework. It was so thick we couldn't even have stuck our hands through it and done the play in braille.

You have to be very tactful with designers. They are the most temperamental of all theater people. They fall madly in love with their own sets and they have very little interest in the actors, the plot, or the play. And they don't like suggestions.

I had a designer my first season at Princeton University, when I ran a summer theater there, who had an invariable built-in reflex that instantly killed any possible criticism. If you made even the slightest suggestion about one of his sets, perhaps the colors could be a little darker or maybe the door a little wider, he instantly and instinctively threw up. It was the single most definitive reaction I have ever known. He didn't do it deliberately; that's just the way it happened. But it certainly made you think twice about making any suggestions. I made one or two tentative ones and ruined two neckties and I never opened my mouth for the rest of the season. Needless to say, we didn't have him back the following year.

The designer at Cleveland, fortunately, didn't throw up; he simply wouldn't give up.

"You've seen the play," I told him. "The entire second act takes place on the balcony. Obviously the latticework will have to go.

"It can't go," he said.

"It will have to."

"I love it," he said.

"I think it's very nice too. And it would be lovely in some other play. But not this one."

"It can't go," he said. "It's holding up the ceiling."

"Then something else will have to hold up the ceiling. The latticework has to go."

"It's not going," he said.

"Let me put it this way," I said. "If it's not going, we are."

I called out to Gloria, who was sitting in the auditorium looking gloomily at the set.

"Go home, Miss Swanson," I said.

This was a little act we had rehearsed to use when theaters were difficult. It was in Gloria's contract that she had sole and total approval of the set, the lights, the props, and everything to do with the physical production wherever we played. Sometimes they refused to give it to us. We were playing summer stock and we were really not unreasonable but sometimes, as in this case, what we were asking for was obligatory.

"Go home, Miss Swanson," went our little act.

"Aren't we going to open?" (Wide-eyed surprise)

"I don't think so." (An Erich von Stroheim reading)

And home we would go to await improvements, which invariably occurred.

This time Gloria didn't even bother with the act. When I said, "Go home, Miss Swanson," she said:

"Well, I should damn well think so," and we went immediately back to her hotel.

We received several frantic phone calls from the producer who, not having seen the play, foolishly backed up the designer. I find that designers have a knack of intimidating the people they work for. We were adamant that we had no intention of trying to play a whole act behind a latticework wall. It would be like trying to do it with the curtain down. The producer threatened to sue us and bring us up on charges at Equity, and it was finally left that we would all talk to Equity in the morning.

Although Gloria and I called from breakfast at five minutes after ten the next morning the producer had reached them first and Equity was not very helpful. They explained to Gloria that she could not refuse to appear under any circumstances; that she did indeed have a clause in her contract guaranteeing her approval of the set, but that all she could do would be to file charges against the producer for violation of contract and the producer would probably be reprimanded and possibly even fined at some later date.

Gloria is a strong lady under any circumstances and absolutely immovable when she knows she is right.

"I made a lot of money before I was a member of Actors Equity," she told them, "and I can do it all over again. You are supposed to protect me and you are not doing so. The point of the rider in my contract is not to get someone a slap on the wrist at some later date. The point of the rider is to protect me from looking stupid in front of the people who pay to see me. I have an obligation to the people who pay to see me and I am not walking on that stage until I am able to fulfill that obligation."

She hung up the phone. It was scarcely back on the hook when it rang again.

It was the producer from the theater.

"Marvelous news, Mr. Kennedy. The latticework is gone."

It was indeed gone and the ceiling didn't fall down and we played out the week and broke the house record for summer stock.

In 1943 I had a wonderful idea for Gloria and myself which turned out to be the best thing we ever did together. I put together an evening of three short plays, one by Shaw, one by Barrie, and one by Pinero, and we called the evening *Three Curtains*. Out of the authors' stage directions and various other of their writings, and with considerable embellishment of my own, I compiled a prologue for each author to speak before the curtain of his own play. The speeches were delivered through three life-sized and very striking masks grouped together over the center of the proscenium.

The three plays were Shaw's *The Man of Destiny*, Barrie's *The Old Lady Shows Her Medals*, and Pinero's *The Playgoers*. The same two stars played the principal roles in all three plays. In *The Old Lady*, Gloria gave what I thought was the best performance of her life. She still thinks her Sadie Thompson in the silent film version of *Rain* was the best thing she's ever done, with *The Old Lady* second, and *Sunset Boulevard* surprisingly only third.

Three Curtains got some very exciting notices on the road and should have come into New York. It didn't for two reasons: we didn't have any money and we did have Francis Lederer.

Francis Lederer was a Czechoslovakian actor who made his

Broadway debut in a play called *Autumn Crocus* wearing lederhosen and oozing Czech charm. He became an instant matinee idol but he was no favorite with his leading lady, Dorothy Gish, who complained that in scenes where she was supposed to be on the stage alone, playing a tender moment, Francis would come on and busy himself polishing the brass on the bar, dusting and clearing the tables.

"But naturally," Francis explained, "I am the owner of the hotel. It is logical that I would always be busy about the place."

Our troubles with Francis, which were considerable, came to a head the night after the opening in Boston. The show got generally good notices and Gloria and I got excellent ones but for some reason Francis did not come off as well. It was surprising, as he was extremely effective and especially as the Scots soldier in the Barrie play, which one might have expected to be the most difficult for him.

But even in that one we had trouble with him. For some reason, all during the play, he was constantly spitting on the floor and it drove Gloria crazy and I think the audience too. I spoke very firmly to him about it and said he would have to stop it.

"But why?" he asked. "I am a soldier. A soldier would spit on the floor."

"Francis, I'm not interested in any esoteric reasons," I said. "American audiences don't like actors to spit on the floor. For good or bad, you're in America, so don't spit on the floor."

"You are worse than Katharine Cornell," he said. He had appeared with Miss Cornell in a road tour of *No Time for Comedy*. "At least she had some excuse because it used to get on the hem of her gowns."

The night after the opening in Boston when I made my entrance in the first play, *Man of Destiny*, I did exactly what I had always done. I was supposed to pound offstage on the locked door of the inn, bellowing and shouting and demanding admission. Francis, as the young Napoleon, was eventually supposed to open the door for me. I bellowed, pounded, and hollered exactly as I always had done, but when Francis finally opened the door and I walked on stage, he looked at me and said:

"Oh, you have read the notices; you are now the star of the play."

I couldn't believe it. Neither could the audience. Neither could Gloria, who was waiting to make her entrance from the other side of the stage. But at least it gave her an inkling of what to expect.

She came on the stage at the top of a flight of steps and said her first line to Francis as she was supposed to.

"Myah, myah, myah," said Francis, mimicking her rhythm.

Gloria stood at the top of the stairs and looked down at him.

"If you open your mouth again," she said, "I will give you such a slap in the face."

He didn't open it again except to say what he was supposed to say, and somehow we got through the evening. The audience was in a state of shock. They didn't know whether they were at a play or a prize fight. It happened that Elliot Norton, the dean of the Boston critics, was in the audience, having come to see the play again to do a Sunday column. He came backstage just as Gloria in tears was shouting, "I will never walk on the stage with that man again."

So the next day the whole story was on the front page of the the Boston *Post* under Elliot's byline with a banner headline reading "Backstage Row Threatens to Close Play."

Francis really flipped when he read that front-page story and forced his way into Gloria's suite when we were having a late supper. We had a most unpleasant and unhappy scene. When he left, escorted by a hotel detective, Gloria and I decided to close the play on Saturday night.

So New York never got to see her do *The Old Lady*. They still may some day if I have my way.

A Goose for the Gander was the Broadway play I wrote for Gloria and she bribed me into writing it.

Gloria was keenly aware of the success of the three prologues I had written for *Three Curtains*. I considered it a great compliment that no critic on the road had ever questioned that they had not in fact been written by Mr. Shaw, Mr. Barrie, and Sir Arthur Wing Pinero. Gloria had been greatly impressed with the writing. She knew, too, that I had majored in playwriting at the Yale Drama School and that I had twice won the undergraduate playwriting prize at Dartmouth, once beating out Budd Schulberg for first place and one other time having been beaten out by him.

So one day when we were playing *Let Us Be Gay* she said to me:

"Your dialogue at Sardi's bar is better than what we have in the play. Why should Rachel Crothers get all those royalties? You write me a play and if you write it I'll guarantee to get it on."

"I don't want to write a play," I said. I was now completely sold on acting and directing.

"I know all your weaknesses," said Gloria, "and I'll make you a deal. If you will lock yourself in your room every day and write from eleven A.M. until six in the afternoon I will come by in the car every night at six and take you to any restaurant in New York, any theater, any nightclub. We'll stay out as late as you want just so long as you're back at the typewriter at eleven the next morning."

I guess I'm a whore at heart; it sounded irresistible. So I locked myself in my room at the Royalton Hotel where Kirk Douglas was the elevator boy and where George Jean Nathan lived and where Julie Haydon used to skip through the lobby and bring him a fresh red rose every morning. In three weeks I had finished the play. It was a lonely three weeks except for the jazzy evenings where I saw all the best plays in town. But in the daytime, when I was writing, my phone never rang even once. One day when I was tired of writing, I thought gloomily, "Is it possible that in this whole vast city there is not a single soul who wants to speak to me?" So I called down to the switchboard and said, "Haven't there been any calls for me?"

A Goose for Gloria Swanson

"Oh, yes, quite a few," said the operator cheerfully, "but Miss Swanson told us not to put them through."

A Goose for the Gander opened at Brattle Hall in Cambridge, Massachusetts, on June 6, 1944. It was quite a day for me. It was the opening night of my first play. It was also my birthday. And, incidentally, it was D-Day.

The Boston notices weren't very good but they weren't bad, either. They made it sound like fun, which it was. I had tailored it totally to Gloria and it was exactly what her audience wanted to see her do. Hardly Chekhov or Ibsen, but her audience was glad it wasn't and they came in droves and we set an all-time house record.

We opened on Broadway at the Playhouse Theatre in January of 1945 and the reaction of the New York critics was best summed up by the New York *Times*, which had a big headline saying: " 'A Goose for the Gander'—Dead Duck."

Robert Coleman on the *Daily Mirror* wrote: "Mr. Kennedy is a kind of Sheboygan Noël Coward." Only the *Post* was relatively kind. It described the play as "hammock reading," which I thought was a reasonable evaluation.

We had in the play on Broadway, in addition to Gloria and myself and Conrad Nagel, a most unusual blond young lady named Choo Choo Johnson. She was statuesque, ample in all departments, and had the most monumental frontal equipment I have ever seen. They used to come on stage like headlights seconds before she got there.

Choo Choo, for obvious reasons, had been the star of Mike Todd's review *Star and Garter* but she told us she was making her legitimate stage debut in our play. I think it is possibly safe to say that not only was *A Goose for the Gander* the first play she had ever been in, it may very well be the only one she had ever seen or read. Anyway, her mental development had not quite kept pace with her physical. But, then, how could it?

The night after the reviews came out, Choo Choo came into my dressing room.

"Listen," she said, "what did Robert Coleman call you?"

I said he had called me a Sheboygan Noël Coward.

"Oh," said Choo Choo. "Is that good or bad?"

Singlehandedly Choo Choo was responsible for the biggest spontaneous laugh I have ever heard in a theater. During the war years Western Union had a difficult time recruiting messengers and Choo Choo was playing the part of a call girl who had decided to answer a Western Union ad and use the service for her own devices. Wearing a low-cut seductive dress with the telegrams tucked inside her considerable cleavage, Choo Choo would deliver telegrams to wealthy men. We got a lot of laughs out of her two short scenes and I used to get a howl on her entrance when she said, "I'm from Western Union," and I would look her up and down and say, "What hath God wrought?"

One night Choo Choo came on for her second scene near the end of the play and we played the scene as usual until we came to the part near the end where I had to cross to her and say, "Give me the telegram."

I said the line just as I always had but when I looked at Choo Choo she had the most terrifying expression on her face. It is an expression not unfamiliar to those of us who act on the stage. It is a kind of wild, dazed, glazed look. When you see this look in another actor's eyes, you know that not only does he not know what the next line is, he doesn't know what play he's in or even what town he's in. It has happened to all of us.

I couldn't believe Choo Choo didn't know her lines, which were painfully simple. Then I quickly realized what the problem was. She must have forgotten the telegram. Now there was no way for the play to go on without that telegram. I had to read it aloud to Gloria and it tied up all the loose ends of the plot. There was no way for me as a character to know what was in the telegram without reading it. No way for Gloria to know. No way to let the audience know. We had to have that telegram.

I tried to think of everything I could. However, there is something I have learned in thirty-seven years on the stage. If

[48]

Detective Story—*Barry Nelson, Rita Gam, Robert Strauss (seated), and assorted detectives in rehearsal.*

Gloria Swanson with Harold J. Kennedy in the 1961 production of The Inkwell.

*Gloria Swanson
and Harold J. Kennedy
in the 1945 Broadway
production of*
A Goose for the Gander.

*Gloria Swanson and
Harold J. Kennedy in
the Pocono Playhouse
production of*
The Inkwell.

From the Pocono Playhouse production of The Inkwell.

Gloria Swanson and Harold J. Kennedy in the 1967 Chicago production of Reprise (*also known as* The Inkwell).

Luise Rainer in the Hollywood production of Joan of Lorraine. *(Photo by Wilson Millar)*

Margaret Sullavan and Joseph Cotten in the 1958 production of Sabrina Fair. *(Photo by Vandamm)*

Tallulah Bankhead. (Photo from the private collection of Cal Schumann)

Above, the 1961 production of
Bell, Book and Candle.
*Seated left to right,
Peter Waldren,
Harold J. Kennedy,
and Ginger Rogers.
Standing, with
hairpiece, William Marshall.*

*Left, Ginger Rogers
and Peter Waldren
in* Bell, Book and Candle.

an actor is in trouble and you try too hard to help him out you usually wind up in even more trouble yourself. It always looks like your fault. So, partly out of self-protection, partly because I couldn't think of anything else to say, and mostly out of desperation, I stood my ground.

"You give me that telegram," I said firmly to her.

Poor Choo Choo. She looked sadly down in that deep cleavage and said wistfully:

"There's nothing there."

Fortunately the audience laughed so loud and so long that it gave Choo Choo a chance to collect herself. She was really quite marvelous. When the audience finally subsided she said:

"I forgot the telegram but I remember what it said." And, completely from memory, she recited the whole telegram that I was supposed to read, tied up all the loose ends of the play, brought the curtain down happily, and got the audience safely into the bars by eleven o'clock.

The Broadway run of A *Goose for the Gander* was the first and only time I ever met Joseph P. Kennedy.

One night after a performance of the play in New York there was a knock at my dressing room door. I opened it to a very distinguished-looking gentleman standing there.

"Mr. Kennedy," he said, "I'm Joseph P. Kennedy and I just came back to tell you that at least ten people have come up to me in the lobby and told me how good my son was in the play."

I also met one of Gloria's ex-husbands, the Marquis Henri de la Falaise de Coudray; he was a delightful man. He had been married to both Gloria and Constance Bennett and he told a story at Gloria's at cocktails one day that I have never forgotten. It was how Constance Bennett had saved his life at Dunkirk.

Henri was very active during the war and much decorated. Being married to both Gloria and Constance Bennett alone might have won him the Croix de Guerre. In any event, he had manned one of the small boats at Dunkirk. According to Henri, during the height of the invasion his small craft capsized and threw him into a turbulent stream that was dragging him away from the shore. He was so tired, he said, so without sleep and totally exhausted, that the water closing over his head seemed almost like a comfortable blanket and he was inclined just to sink back under it and rest forever. He went down twice with no real feeling of discomfort but when he was starting to go down for the third time he got a mental picture of Constance Bennett at his funeral in a black hat and veil and two hundred pearls, saying, "My poor Henri, he died a hero," and he said to himself:

"That bitch. I'm not going to let her get away with it."

So, using Constance's face like a mechanical rabbit, he swam safely to the shore.

A Goose for the Gander closed after only two weeks in New York. The theater had been previously booked for a play Brock Pemberton was doing about an invisible rabbit. We had many a laugh over what a preposterous idea that was. Our producer, Jules Leventhal, the king of the subway circuit, was willing to take a gamble and move our play to another theater. But, Gloria had somehow found the time during our two-week run to marry her sixth husband, William Davey, and she decided she was going to be a housewife.

That turned out to be a bad idea on all counts and in a few months we were off on the road again where we played the play for thirty more weeks. It was also a great favorite in summer stock. Guy Palmerton, the dean of the summer theater producers, presented it three different times at his theater at Fitchburg, Massachusetts, twice in legitimate productions with Gloria and me, and once in a contraband production with his own company and a different title invented in the hope I wouldn't find out about it and he wouldn't have to pay me any royalty. That was a favorite trick of some summer stock producers. They would change the name of *Little Lord Fauntleroy* to *Sex on Sunday* for two reasons. One, they figured it would sell more tickets, and, two, they wouldn't have to pay the author's royalty.

Just as Gloria was beginning to wear out her welcome slightly in summer stock and as the legend was beginning to diminish, she went back to Hollywood and re-created it.

Gloria tells about the first supposedly sneak preview of *Sunset Boulevard*, which was attended by everyone who was anyone in Hollywood. Gloria was in the fourth row. When the picture ended there was absolute total silence. She started to sneak up the aisle. And then the ovation started. And the cheers. As she got halfway up the aisle, one of the great ladies of Hollywood—Gloria still isn't sure whether it was Barbara Stanwyck or Loretta Young—knelt in front of her and said, "And still the Queen!" She was.

She came back to Broadway that same year and co-starred with Jose Ferrer in a smash hit revival of *Twentieth Century*. She was at the top again.

After that I sent her out on a long summer tour of a play by Andrew Rosenthal called *Red Letter Day* with Buddy Rogers and Lois Wilson, which I produced and directed but which I couldn't tour with because I was running my own summer theater, the Grist Mill Playhouse at Andover, New Jersey.

In 1962 I wrote another play for her, this time not because she asked me to or bribed me into it, but because I wanted to and had to write it for her. It was a play about all the lady stars I have known and worked with: the glamour, the guts, the strength, the possessiveness, and yet deep down that silent inner loneliness that I have so often found. It was a play that could be seen on two levels. You could go and have a light frothy evening, which many people did, or you could go and listen to what the play had to say, which many other people did. Gloria and I received countless letters from people to whom it meant a great deal. I will never forget a beautiful letter we received from a woman in Chicago who wrote that her husband had died five months before and that the night she saw our play was the first night since his death that she had gone home and turned the key in the apartment door without bursting into tears.

When I first started writing, D. A. Doran, then the story editor at Paramount, said to me, "Always remember that the greatest fear in life is the fear of loneliness." I have never forgotten it.

We have played the play on and off almost everywhere for the last ten years and I think it is because of its theme and because of Gloria's performance that we have had standing ovations almost everywhere. We were cowards not to bring it to New York. It would have been rewarding even for one night.

My happiest recollection of that play, originally called *The Inkwell* and finally *Reprise,* is of doing the corny song and dance with which Gloria and I wound up the play. Playing two mismated souls, who because of their individual problems could be of no real help to each other, we were desperately trying to cheer each other up doing an imitation of Janet Gaynor and Charles Farrell in *Sunnyside Up.*

One night in our last engagement at the Huntington Hartford Theatre in Hollywood when the play was going especially well and the audience had come in as Moss Hart used to say, "laughing at the ushers," Gloria sat on my knee and before she started to sing she leaned over and kissed me.

"I never want to act with anybody but you," she said.

It would suit me fine.

She is a lady who has always been honest about her age as she has been about everything else. She was born in 1899, so she is always one year older than the year we are living in. She is seventy-nine now and seemingly indestructible. I hope she is. I would not like to start a new year without her. Long live the Queen!

JUDITH ANDERSON
AND FLORENCE REED

I ASKED Jean Barrere, stage manager for Judith Anderson's highly acclaimed Broadway revival of *Medea*, whether Miss Anderson used any particular acting method.

"Judith has her own method," Jean said. "She drives herself into a frenzy before she walks on the stage."

He pointed out that her very first entrance in the play where she comes on shrieking, "Death! DEATH!" is at an emotional peak few actresses are able to reach by the end of a normal third act. He then told me a story about Judith and her arch enemy, Florence Reed, who was co-starring in the play with her along with John Gielgud.

When Jean called "half hour" one night, Judith Anderson called him into her dressing room and said:

"I want you to take this message to Florence Reed. You are to tell that old bitch that she is not to move a muscle, not a muscle, during my soliloquy. Now tell her that exactly."

Jean then went and knocked on Florence's door. "Come in,"

said Florence in that deep Mother Goddam voice. He opened the door and there was Florence adjusting her chin straps and putting on a gallon of rouge.

"I have a message from Miss Anderson," Jean said, and repeated the message verbatim.

Florence gave one of the chin straps an extra tug. "Tell Judith," she said, "to go fuck herself."

Jean did what we all do under those circumstances, which is nothing. He called "fifteen minutes," then "five minutes," and finally "places" and no questions were asked.

Florence took her place on the stage and the curtain went up.

Meantime Judith was pacing like a panther in the wings waiting for her entrance.

As she passed the stage manager's desk she said to Jean, "Did you give Florence my message?"

"Yes, Miss Anderson," said Jean. "Warning. You're on."

"What did she say?" demanded Judith.

"You're on, Miss Anderson."

"Tell me what she said," hissed Judith, already in character.

"She said, Miss Anderson, that you should go fuck yourself."

"DEATH!" screamed Judith. "DEATH!" And plummeted onto the stage.

LUISE OF LORRAINE

LUISE RAINER HAS a look of perpetual surprise, as though she had been unexpectedly but not unpleasantly goosed. She prefaces everything she says with a long "Oooooh," which is, I suppose, a kind of verbal acknowledgment of the digital salute.

I took her back to Hollywood to make her Los Angeles stage debut in the starring role of Maxwell Anderson's *Joan of Lorraine*, which she had played for me at Princeton University and in which she could be quite brilliant. I say could be because she wasn't always. It depended on the pauses. In the matter of pauses Luise was the most self-indulgent actress I have ever worked with. When a beat of two would be more than sufficient, she would take a beat of twelve. Of course she was perfect casting as Joan and she may have been listening to voices of her own, but the audience couldn't hear them and during the longer pauses you could go to the bar and have a drink, which people sometimes did.

Luise is not a great one to take direction. In Hollywood

[55]

(where she won two Oscars) the director has more clout than he does in summer stock. He can also cut at his own discretion. In our production the pauses remained totally unpredictable.

Early in rehearsal in Hollywood, Luise sent me a message through the director, Jus Addiss, who had been the stage manager of Ingrid Bergman's Broadway production of the play.

"Luise asked me to speak to you," said Jus. "She says you seem to think the Dauphin is a comedy part."

"I certainly do," I said. "And so did Maxwell Anderson. And so did Romney Brent, who played it in New York."

"Miss Rainer doesn't want laughs," Jus said. "She says they disturb the rhythm of the play."

"You can tell Luise," I said, "that if I don't get laughs as the Dauphin I am going to kill myself and I am going to leave a suicide note blaming her."

Luise and I didn't speak much after that.

The play opened at the Ivar Theatre in Hollywood and Luise got distinctly divided notices. Some said she was brilliant, which was true. Others said she was overly indulgent, which was also true.

Luise is really no worse than many other brilliant people I have worked with. Some of them are genuinely gifted, super talented, and know a great deal, but they might qualify for what Homer Curran once sadly observed about Ruth Chatterton: "She knows so much, she really does, that it's a great pity she thinks she knows just a little bit more than she does know."

I am not one to take pauses. I am of the old George Abbott school of pick-up-the-pace-and-get-on-with-it. Whether it was because the part was so good, or because I was genuinely right for it, or because I picked up a distinctly faltering pace, my own notices as the Dauphin were unanimous raves.

Patterson Greene in the Los Angeles *Examiner* wrote: "Mr. Kennedy's Dauphin is something of a masterpiece: cynical, amusing, evil"; and unfortunately the Los Angeles *Times* concluded a three-paragraph pan of Luise by saying: "But I was delighted by Mr. Kennedy's portrayal of the Dauphin."

Naturally this didn't set too well with Luise. At the theater the second night the notices were never mentioned and Luise and I spoke only on stage. On the third night there was a sold-out house.

Luise and I were discovered on stage—there was no curtain in the play—as part of a group of actors preparing to rehearse a play about Saint Joan. When the house lights dimmed and it was time for the play to start, an actor playing the role of the director of the play barked out orders to us from the front of the house. He had some caustic dialogue and when he came to his first funny line, the packed audience howled with laughter.

"Ooooh," she said. "They are goons tonight. It will be your night."

As the run went on the pauses got longer and longer. The stage manager finally had to speak very sharply to Luise, as we were running into overtime for the stagehands and patrons were missing the last bus to Pasadena.

Even Luise's most ardent fans seemed vaguely aware that the evening was somewhat longer than *Parsifal* and without the music. Two contented customers were sitting in front of a friend of mine one night and when the play was over they rose to their feet in ecstasy.

"Wasn't it wonderful," they said, "wasn't she marvelous? Oh God, I hope the bars are still open."

Toward the end of the run when business wasn't as good as we had hoped Luise had the misfortune to develop a genuine case of laryngitis and for the last four performances she refused to go on unless I went before the curtain and explained this to the audience.

"Ladies and gentlemen," I was instructed to say, "Miss Rainer has laryngitis and is under doctor's orders not to play this performance—(Huge groan)—However—(Breathless silence)—this brave little trouper will appear regardless." (Ovation.)

[57]

MIRIAM HOPKINS

MIRIAM HOPKINS IS REPUTED to have given Bette Davis her first gray hairs, and I wouldn't doubt it. They did two highly successful films together at Warner Brothers but apparently both were bathed in blood.

Miriam could be pure enchantment once you got the ground rules settled. She was doing John Van Druten's play *There's Always Juliet* for me at Princeton in 1947, and the only time she and I ever tangled was in the early stages of rehearsal. I was playing a small but terribly good part with a number of very funny lines. It was to be my first appearance of the season at Princeton and I had worked very hard on it. I also knew where the good lines were.

One day at rehearsal I was sitting on the couch balancing a martini, as you always do in those plays, and I was just about to time my funniest line when I saw and heard Miriam starting to dust the piano.

"Are you going to do that?" I asked her.

[58]

"Well, I have to do something," Miriam said.

"You might just stand still and listen," I suggested.

"Suppose I don't want to?" she asked.

"Don't forget," I said, "I am also the director of this play. If you move on one of my laugh lines I simply raise a finger and the entire bank of pink lights goes out."

"You bitch," she said. "I bet you'd do it."

"You bet your ass I would," I said. She fell, laughing, into my arms and was heaven ever after.

As is often the case with lady stars, we were rehearsing at Miriam's apartment in New York. It was a gorgeous apartment on Sutton Place and we had the use of all of Miriam's expensive furniture, which suited the play perfectly but which turned out to be a mistake. These ladies get easily spoiled and when Miriam got to Princeton and saw the furniture we were going to use in the actual production it was substantially south of her heart's desire.

"I can't act on this second-hand junk," she said.

I explained to her the difficulty in borrowing first-rate furniture and props in a small town like Princeton.

"Don't you have a truck?" she asked. I said we did.

"Then it's very simple," said Miriam. "Send the truck to New York and take the furniture out of my apartment."

I couldn't believe it but she got right on the backstage phone and called her maid. She said that a truck would be arriving in two hours and that the maid was to let them take everything out of the living room, the couch, the chairs, the lamps, whatever. Then she hung up, but called back immediately with an afterthought.

"If my husband is asleep on the couch, which he usually is," she told the maid, "be sure to get him off it before they move it."

"We don't need him down here," she said as she hung up.

Princeton was the opening of a ten-week summer tour for Miriam. When I saw her at the end of the summer she told me what a wonderful tour she had had.

"But nobody gave me the physical production you gave me," she said. "Yours was gorgeous."

She had completely forgotten that it was totally her own.

Years later I invited her to play the mother in *The Front Page* on Broadway. I wrote her in Hollywood and told her to call me collect. She did call.

"But I'm not calling collect," she said, "because I'm not going to do it. I just don't think the part is good enough."

It was subsequently played by Helen Hayes, Maureen O'Sullivan, Dody Goodman, and Julia Meade.

The last time I saw Miriam she came over to my table at Sardi's and said, "Well, everybody did it but me. I'm not very bright. It's the story of my life."

She died in Hollywood a few months later.

MARGARET SULLAVAN

JOSEPH COTTEN, WHO IS an old friend from the Mercury Theatre days and who always has an iced Beefeater martini ready for me when I go to Hollywood or when he is passing through New York, is responsible for one of the most rewarding experiences I have ever had in the theater.

Through Jo I was privileged to sponsor Margaret Sullavan's return to acting after an unhappy retirement and a year in a sanitarium. In 1957 at the peak of her career Miss Sullavan was slated to appear in an hour television show aired live from New York. She completed the dress rehearsal an hour before the scheduled airing, walked out of the studio, presumably to get a sandwich, and was never seen again. The hour was filled with some distinctly uneasy organ music.

What I was told, and what I believe, is that the talk-back mike in the control room was inadvertently left open and that as Miss Sullavan was leaving the sound stage she heard a voice saying:

[61]

"We'll never make that old bag look forty."

There was considerable furor in the papers and no one, not even her agent or her husband, would admit to knowing where she was. A few months later one of the tabloids discovered her in a private nursing home in Stockbridge, Massachusetts, where she was known merely as "Mag, the Wag" to the other patients.

In the late spring of 1958 I received a call from an agent asking whether I would be interested in presenting Margaret Sullavan and Joseph Cotten in their Broadway hit *Sabrina Fair* at my Grist Mill Playhouse. I said I would indeed be interested but that I knew for a fact that Jo Cotten was not available, as I had already written him and had received a letter just two days before saying he really didn't want to play summer stock.

"The situation is different now," the agent explained. "Miss Sullavan, as you know, has been ill and now she wants to find out whether she still has what it takes to work on the stage. She thinks summer stock would be the place to find out. But she won't do the play without Jo. So when I explained it to Jo he said that under these circumstances of course he would do it. He also said he would not play anywhere unless we first played for you. So that's why I'm calling."

I didn't ask what it cost. "I'll take it," I said.

"In all fairness I must warn you," the agent said. "You know the history. And there is always a chance."

"I'll take it," I said.

Margaret Sullavan had always been my favorite actress. I had seen her movies when I was an undergraduate at Dartmouth. I saw all four performances of the George S. Kaufman–Edna Ferber play *Stage Door* when she tried it out, prior to Broadway at the Shubert Theatre in New Haven when I was a student at the Yale Drama School. Later, in New York, I saw countless performances of *The Voice of the Turtle*, taking every visiting fireman to share this special treat with them. And then there were *The Deep Blue Sea* and *Janus* and others.

I wrote a short note to Miss Sullavan, whom I had never

met, saying how pleased I was to be presenting her at my theater and explaining that I was basically an actor and that I
hoped she would come to us secure in the thought that she
would be surrounded by complete understanding and deep admiration and affection.

She had a history of hating management, as many actors do.
She broke a mirror over the head of her company manager,
Sammy Schwartz, before a matinee of *The Voice of the Turtle*
in New York one day and then sent her maid at intermission to find out if he was going to take her out to dinner as
usual.

The company rehearsed in New York, where the stage manager of the Broadway production was reproducing the original
staging. We were lucky enough also to have Cathleen Nesbitt
and Luella Gear from the Broadway cast. As I was not directing it, I wisely stayed away from rehearsals. But I did take Miss
Sullavan and Jo to lunch one day at Sardi's. She seemed in very
high spirits, looked eighteen, ate ravenously, and seemed to
enjoy my stories about the rigors of summer stock.

When the cast arrived at Andover Sunday afternoon for the
dress rehearsal Sunday night, my cousin Claire prepared a quite
marvelous cold buffet which we served them in my apartment
over the theater as soon as they got out of their cars. Miss
Sullavan came—Jo had said she probably wouldn't—and she
seemed very nervous but quietly so and was apparently in control. She ate very little and after a while she came over to me
in the corner and said, "I know I don't have to explain to you
but I have to be by myself for a while."

We didn't see her again until the dress rehearsal, though several of the actors reported seeing her walking by herself in the
fields and along the lovely country roads outside the little
town. I couldn't help wondering what that lady was thinking
about. A genuine superstar in every medium and then a year in
a sanitarium. And now, would it come back or wouldn't it? I
think she knew less than any of us.

I had tried to make everything perfect for this production.

[63]

We had spent a great deal of time and money on the set and I had tried to have every prop exactly right. I was apprehensive when she walked in from the front of the theater to look at the set.

"It's better than the New York set," she said simply. "You've done everything right. Now I guess it's up to me."

Dress rehearsal went without a hitch and I drove Miss Sullavan home to the old farmhouse where she was staying. "Thank you for everything," she said as she got out of the car. And that was all.

We didn't see her, even on the country roads, all the next day, the day of the opening, and I must admit it worried me.

"Don't worry," Jo said. "She'll be here."

"It sounds corny," I told him, "but I really care more for her than I do for me."

"I knew you would," said Jo. "That's the reason I insisted we open here."

I didn't see her again until she walked on the stage that night. "Hello, Hello," called Sabrina offstage in that unmistakable voice and the applause started. When she hit the stage there was an ovation. When it quieted down she said her first lines and I knew it was there. But the revelation came after she said a few more lines. And then *she* knew it. I could see her knowing it, disbelieving it for a minute, then tasting it and savoring it. "Glittering" she had been described in that performance in New York. And "incandescent." She was more than that that night. Everything she had ever had that had gone away had come back and come back in full flower.

As soon as the curtain fell after countless curtain calls I went back and knocked on her dressing room door.

"It's you," she said. "I hoped it would be."

"Were you surprised?" I asked.

She nodded her head very slowly and she was crying.

"I wasn't," I said.

"I know," she said and kissed me. "And now I think you should start calling me Maggie."

GUY MADISON IN "JOHN LOVES JOHN"

Guy Madison came to Princeton in 1948 and played *John Loves Mary* for me. That was in the days before stars traveled with full packages. Today a star traveling in summer stock carries his full cast with him even down to the tiniest bit. But at that time each theater had a resident company of actors and the star traveled alone, sending ahead an advance director who played his part in rehearsals and directed the company in all of the proper moves and stage business. Then the star would arrive on Sunday, rehearse Sunday afternoon, Sunday night, and again Monday afternoon, and if the advance director had done his job properly the whole performance was pretty well melded by the opening night on Monday.

Guy arrived on Sunday afternoon and we went immediately into rehearsal. Things were going extremely well until we reached a point where Mr. Madison sat unexpectedly on the couch beside me. When we had rehearsed the play he had presumably been on the other side of the stage. We had a rule

[65]

that you never stopped rehearsal so I kept on going, but I did feel obligated to break the rule a few minutes later when, after a long pause, Mr. Madison looked into my eyes and said quite firmly, "I love you."

Now this wouldn't surprise anyone in today's theater. But this was Princeton, New Jersey, in 1948 and I felt we should go no further.

"Herbert," I said to the director, "is he going to say that to me?"

"Guy," said Herbert gently. "You are supposed to say that to Mary."

"I know," said Guy, "but Mary is supposed to be on the couch."

TALLULAH

TALLULAH BANKHEAD WAS a marvelous woman. Everything that has been said about her is true, I suppose, and she would be the last to deny it, but no one has ever captured Tallulah on paper and no one ever will. You had to know her and be with her, not just in the living room or the barroom but also working with her and listening to her, which was mandatory, and laughing with her, which was easy, and then put her gently to bed at night, which is what I remember most of all.

Yes, she was a nonstop talker, but Tallulah was never boring. When she told stories about the famous personalities she knew like Winston Churchill she wasn't just repeating what you and she had both read in *Time* magazine, she was telling a private and intimate story that was revealing, always perceptive, and often touching.

She was a big drinker, but she never drank before a performance. She did five plays for me, *Private Lives, The Second Mrs. Tanqueray, Her Cardboard Lover, The Little Foxes,* and *Wel-*

come, Darlings and she was brilliant and totally disciplined in every one of them. As a matter of fact, she gave a performance in Pinero's *The Second Mrs. Tanqueray* that was one of the greatest acting performances I have ever seen. If I had not been such a neophyte in the theater at the time I would have stolen the money to bring it to Broadway, which might have changed my life and maybe Tallulah's too.

Welcome, Darlings was a hodgepodge of a revue which had been put together as a vehicle for Tallulah in summer stock. It contained two of my favorite Tallulahisms in a hilarious sketch where Tallulah played Peter Pan.

In lines taken directly out of the James M. Barrie script, Tallulah as Peter Pan said to Wendy, "What is your name?"

Right out of the Barrie original Wendy replied, "Wendy Moira Angela Darling. What is your name?"

To which Tallulah replied, "Peter Pan, darling."

Then the other reading which rocked the house was when Wendy said to Peter, "Do you really know some fairies?"

Tallulah replied, "I used to, but they're mostly dead now."

When she did *The Second Mrs. Tanqueray* for me at Amherst in 1940 she sent ahead a scrawled note of instructions, among which was a stipulation we couldn't quite figure out. Either it said there must be steps leading up to the center door or it said there must not be. We opted for the former; otherwise why mention it at all? My designer was a boy just out of Ann Arbor in his first professional job in the theater, Lemuel Ayers, later responsible for such Broadway hits as *Oklahoma!* and *Kiss Me, Kate*. He provided a gorgeous set of Victorian steps leading up to a magnificent center door.

When Tallulah arrived it turned out that we were wrong. She screamed the place down when she saw the steps. "I cannot act on steps," she said.

It isn't an easy matter to get rid of a flight of steps on a stage set. You can't just remove them; it will leave the door hanging in the middle of the wall and the only way to get out would be

[68]

to pole-vault. I begged Tallulah to bear with us and after a few soothing martinis she agreed to try the steps.

At dress rehearsal she was brilliant, building a scene of venom and hatred which culminated in her going to the center door, turning on her husband's family, jamming a huge hatpin into her brilliant red hat, and denouncing everybody. She built the scene magnificently and headed warily for the steps. But she was in the full flush of performance and mounted them like a hurricane. And then as she turned front I saw her expression change. There she was towering three feet above the other actors, in total command of everything. She hurled Mrs. Tanqueray's final challenge and swept off the stage.

The steps were never mentioned again. But as I passed her dressing room the next night I heard her giving instructions to her advance director who was preceding the company to the next stop, Ogunquit, Maine.

"And, darling, tell them I must have steps. I cannot act without steps."

Tallulah always knew what she wanted and wasn't particularly tractable if she didn't get it. All her stock contracts always provided that she must have footlights. I always gave them to her. But she left an especially happy engagement for me at the Grist Mill Playhouse and went on to Westport, where they refused to give her footlights, so she threw all the furniture off the stage and had to be physically dissuaded from throwing the producer after it.

Tallulah came down to Philadelphia to see a Thursday matinee of Orson's production of *Five Kings* because her then husband, John Emery, was playing Hotspur. *Five Kings* was a combination and, fortunately, a condensation of five of Shakespeare's chronicle plays and Orson was playing Falstaff in *Henry IV*. Maurice Evans had already opened as Falstaff in a rival production of *Henry IV* in New York.

[69]

That afternoon Tallulah invited the entire cast to come back to New York after the evening performance for a big bash at her apartment at the Elysee. One of my most vivid recollections of Tallulah is her sitting on the couch at the end of that evening after most of the guests had gone, holding court, stark naked, legs spread far apart, and giving the most brilliant scholarly discussion of the relative values of Orson's Falstaff and that of Maurice Evans. I have studied Shakespeare in two universities and have never heard any famed scholar so eloquent on the subject. Quoting other Shakespeare, quoting obscure authorities, quoting the script itself, Tallulah proved point by point beyond the shadow of a doubt that Orson was ten times better than Maurice Evans.

She then wound up the whole discussion by saying, "Now, mind you, darling, I haven't seen Maurice Evans."

One of the saddest and most endearing things about Tallulah was her inability to get to sleep at night if she were left alone. Whenever she played for me I took her home every night and stayed beside the bed until she was safely and quite soundly asleep.

"Hold my hand," she would say. And I would take it and hold it firmly until gradually it would begin to slip out of my grasp. Then I would start to tiptoe out. But more often than not she would just barely open her eyes and murmur:

"Not yet. Please not yet. It hasn't happened yet."

The utter loneliness of so many of these supposedly strong women has always saddened me. I don't know whether it's because on the way up they are so dedicated to their careers and the idea of making it that on the way down they have nothing to turn to, or whether because of their fame and position and wealth they always attract the wrong kind of people. A little of both I would suspect. I do know that on the way down these ladies attract only the strong self-centered men who want to use them or, inevitably, the gays, who worship them but are of no use to them.

Kay Francis was a beauty on the screen and off. She was a warm, lovely, gracious, and generous woman and at the end she was one of the loneliest women in the world.

Fortunately, and not typically, she never had to worry about money. She had invested wisely and when I took her home one night a little under the weather and very depressed, she took my hand and said, "The one thing I have is that I will never have to worry about money as long as I live." I was greatly reassured by this and indeed when she died, in a typical and I thought quite wonderful gesture, she left a million dollars for the training of seeing-eye dogs.

Kay was not a big drinker and she certainly was not an unpleasant drinker. She simply couldn't drink very well and the liquor invariably went to her legs. She could be sitting with you in a restaurant carrying on a perfectly sensible conversation and get up to go to the ladies' room and fall full on her face.

I remember taking her one night to a little restaurant upstairs in the East Fifties when she fell down and it took three of us, the head waiter, the owner, and myself, to carry her down the stairs and out into the street.

The owner and the maître d' were holding Kay slumped between them while I was trying to hail a cab when a young sailor went by and stared at her.

"Is that Kay Francis?" he said.

Kay half-opened her eyes and smiled that million dollar smile.

"It used to be," she said.

I have known a great number of these ladies in their declining years and unfortunately Kay's case was not exceptional.

But this is not the way they want to be remembered. Back to the brash Tallulah. On one of my lecture tours a critic wrote, "Mr. Kennedy is a kind of masculine Tallulah Bankhead." When I reported this to Tallulah, she said, "A masculine Tallulah Bankhead? Darling, don't be redundant."

She took John Emery and me out on the town one night.

"We're going to get loaded," she said. She was celebrating some victory in Europe for which she felt personally responsible. We went from place to place, the Stork, Twenty-One, and wound up at the old Club 18. We were in a booth for three, all quite smashed, and Tallulah was telling some of her most flavorsome stories. She was extremely loud and she was using language that was unfamiliar even to me.

In the middle of one of her stories I saw a very distinguished white-haired gentleman rise from a table across the room and start toward us.

"Please, God," I thought, "don't let him come here."

As he came nearer the table it was obvious he was a southern colonel if there ever was one. Almost too much so. On the stage you would say he was overdone. Back to wardrobe.

He stopped at the table and bowed.

"Miss Bankhead," he said.

Tallulah was in the midst of a graphic description of one of her earlier sexual exploits. And she turned sharply and glared at him.

"Ah am a friend of your fathah," he said.

Tallulah could be any character she wanted to be any time she wanted to be. She took my mother out for tea once in the garden of the Lord Jeffrey Inn at Amherst and decided to be Rebecca of Sunnybrook Farm. She was better at it than Mary Pickford ever was. And until the day she died my mother was convinced that the stories about Tallulah were libelous and that Tallulah had the vocabulary of a cloistered nun.

Now, she looked at this man and when he said he was a friend of her father she picked her characterization. She was a little southern girl in a swing with magnolias in her hair and in a few minutes I could smell the honeysuckle above the scotch.

She was enchanting. She told him how she had loved her daddy, how she missed him, and how she prayed for him every night.

The colonel was enraptured. But he stayed too long. Tallulah quickly got bored with those characterizations which were too far from home.

As he finally bent over to kiss her hand farewell, she turned to me in triumph and said:

"That ought to hold the old cocksucker."

And there went Rebecca of Sunnybrook Farm.

SINCLAIR LEWIS

SINCLAIR LEWIS WAS a brilliant novelist, but an actor he certainly was not. And, unlike Thornton Wilder, he had no personal charm or special quality to bring to his own work when it was staged.

However, like many writers and indeed many plumbers, he decided he wanted to take to the boards. Everyone in the world wants to act except actors; all actors want to be directors.

Mr. Lewis decided to appear in summer stock in a dramatization of one of his own novels, *It Can't Happen Here,* and he chose the Berkshire Playhouse at Stockbridge, Massachusetts, where I was serving my theater apprenticeship, as his opening date.

It was apparent from the first rehearsal that the whole venture was doomed. I was sitting at the bar in the Red Lion Inn one evening during rehearsals, carefully avoiding any mention of his play and concentrating on the brilliance of his novels, when a young student very courteously approached us, explained to Mr. Lewis that he was a great admirer, and asked most politely for an autograph.

Mr. Lewis—"Red" he had told me to call him—took the piece of paper the boy offered him, wrote something rather lengthy on it and handed the paper to me. It said simply, "Why don't you find a hobby that isn't a nuisance to other people?" and it was unsigned.

The boy was embarrassed and so was I, but the boy got even.

The play opened the following Monday night and was a disaster. Mr. Lewis was sitting gloomily in his dressing room after the curtain had fallen, when a note was hand delivered by an usher.

He opened it and in his own handwriting he read:

"Why don't you find a hobby that isn't a nuisance to other people?"

GINGER

IT SEEMS THAT GINGER ROGERS never smiles. It may be that someone has told her it would crack her face. It may more likely be that she is a lady devoid of one smidgin of one inch of a sense of humor. When other people are falling on the floor with laughter I have heard Ginger say, "That's very amusing." But she says it in much the same tone that Victoria must have said, "We are not amused," and it throws much the same pall.

It's too bad she doesn't have a sense of humor about her husbands, because the one I had to deal with, her fifth, was strictly no laughs, on or off the stage.

I had always admired her as a screen actress and had always wanted her to do a play for me. I had written her many times, receiving no reply, and finally her agent, Louis Shurr, arranged a meeting at her house. He picked me up in his Rolls-Royce and his chauffeur drove us out there. Louis shook all the way out and all through the interview. Ginger was gracious enough —well mannered would be a better description—but I remember thinking even then, and to my great surprise and disappointment, that she was colder than anyone else I had met. Totally unlike her screen self—which only goes to prove what a good actress she is.

It was cocktail time but Ginger doesn't drink liquor and no cocktails were served. Presumably she drinks tea, or Coke, or pink lemonade but none of those was forthcoming either. I did think she could at least serve her poor trembling agent a bicarbonate of soda.

It was agreed that she would do the starring role for me in a ten-week summer tour of John Van Druten's *Bell, Book and Candle,* which Rex Harrison and Lilli Palmer had done on Broadway. And I in turn agreed to get her a salary of $7,500 per week, not inconsiderable in summer stock. She, of course, was to play the Lilli Palmer role and I promised to get her a top-flight leading man and supporting cast.

"I'm sure everything will be just great," Louis said at the door.

"It better be," said Ginger, "or off goes your head."

I hoped that she was kidding, but I gathered from the way Louis shook all the way home that he didn't think she was.

Ginger wasn't married at that time and there was no hint when we discussed the summer plans that anything of that nature was impending. But about a month later I read in the papers that Ginger had taken her fifth husband, a man named G. William Marshall, vaguely described in the papers as a great buddy of Errol Flynn's and a kind of man about Schwab's. There were photographs of Ginger looking girlishly radiant and I had no idea when I was looking at those pictures what that marriage was going to do to *Bell, Book and Candle.*

About a week later I got a call from Ginger.

"I've found my leading man," she said. This rather surprised me, as I hadn't asked her to find one.

"Who is that?" I asked.

"My husband," she said.

"Has he ever been on the stage?"

"No. But he's handsome and charming and he'll be wonderful."

Handsome and charming are matters of opinion. Wonderful he definitely was not. Nor did anyone have any right to expect him to be. Any experienced actor will tell you that light comedy like *Bell, Book and Candle* is far more difficult to act than more substantial plays like *Death of a Salesman* or even Shakespeare. These light comedies require tremendous technical skill in coloring, pacing, and timing that takes years of experience to acquire. Many first-rate actors never do master this special technique. Of American actors, the late Donald Cook was probably the most skillful in this vein and it was no accident that the smart ladies like Tallulah and Gertrude Lawrence always insisted on him as their leading man.

These ladies also realized something that Ginger wasn't aware of, or didn't choose to be. Acting is like a game of tennis and you can't play a good game if there is no one to return the ball. I have never seen Ginger on the stage except in *Bell, Book and Candle*. I am sure she must be a first-rate stage actress, but because of what she saddled herself with in that play at least she had to settle for a very slow game of acting.

The production was doomed from the first minute of the first rehearsal in Detroit. Ginger and Bill were literally still on their honeymoon and it was immediately apparent that they didn't know their lines.

Learning lines is kindergarten work, but it must be done at home, and by yourself, and before rehearsals begin. There are those of the "method" school who say they can't begin to learn their lines until they get the "feel" of the other actors and the sound of their voices, but in the economics of today's theater and the reduced rehearsal time available, this is impractical nonsense. There is too much advanced acting to do in rehearsals—stage business, pacing, timing, handling of props, working with other actors—to waste that time learning lines. I was only allowed a total of ten days' rehearsal time on my Broadway production of *The Front Page* and I could never have done it had not every one of those twenty-four actors come knowing every word of the script.

Most of the Detroit rehearsal time was devoted to nursing Ginger and Bill through their lines. But as they began to learn them, something worse became apparent. There was now reason to hope that Bill would eventually know the words, but there seemed no reason to hope that he would ever know how to say them properly. Rex Harrison he was not.

Sometimes I felt very sorry for him. I think he did try. But it is difficult to stay sorry for someone who has deliberately put himself into a totally untenable position. He was not only doing the play a disservice, he was doing a disservice to himself and to the other actors.

Moss Hart used to say a family is a dynasty ruled over by its weakest member. And I think a play inadvertently comes under the control of its weakest actor.

Luck never rode much with Bill as far as *Bell, Book and Candle* was concerned. At the final dress rehearsal he wore his hairpiece for the first time. When he came through the center door, which was a perfectly normal height, the hairpiece was so pompadoured that the top of the doorframe swept it right off his head and it stayed there swinging on a nail while Bill proceeded to center stage looking as though he had been scalped, which he promptly was by the Detroit critics.

Needless to say, Bill was not prepared to change the hairpiece and we had to rebuild the door an extra foot. It was the highest hairpiece I have ever seen and would have had trouble getting through an arch at St. Patrick's Cathedral. At least he had the sense to try it out at dress rehearsal. Kitty Carlisle played opposite Herbert Berghoff in *Design for Living* in Cleveland and Herbert never wore his hairpiece until the opening night. When Kitty opened the door to let him onstage in the first act she was confronted by a man she had never seen before and promptly closed the door in his face.

The leading Detroit critic wrote after our opening:

"The program lists Mr. Marshall as having been acquainted

[79]

with many phases of show business. Last night he showed not even a nodding acquaintance with any of them."

The other paper implied that Miss Rogers and her husband were charming but not up to the professional standards of the rest of the cast.

The three supporting players, including myself, received unanimously excellent reviews. This didn't help my relationship with Ginger. She came into my dressing room the day after the reviews appeared.

"Congratulations on your notices," she said. And it was the closest I ever came to seeing her smile. That was almost the last conversation we had on the tour.

Unlike Sam Levene, who insists on calling me "Mr. Kennedy" out of respect and genuine affection, Ginger called me Mr. Kennedy as though she were addressing the Führer or Otto Preminger. It was always like a mild slap in the face. Just the tiniest sting.

Actually I understood Ginger very well and she never knew how genuinely sympathetic I was to her. She was very much in love with Bill Marshall at the time and I am a pushover for love on or off the stage. I understand, too, that when we love someone and when that person is inept, it makes us fiercely protective (as I am sure it does with someone who is handicapped). The real problem between Ginger and me was very simple. She knew Bill was no good in the play; she knew that I knew it; and worst of all she knew that I knew that she knew it.

One of their most annoying practices was to speak French to each other in front of the rest of the company on the assumption that we peasants wouldn't know what they were talking about.

One evening at a dress rehearsal in Fitchburg, Massachusetts, Ginger went out to the front of the theater to look at the set and asked Bill to come out on the stage and walk around so that she could see the lighting. As he moved around she called out to him from the front of the house.

Ginger

"Mon cher, fermez la porte de la cuisine."

"Qu'est-ce que c'est, ma petite, ma chère, mon chou-chou?" Bill called back from the stage.

"Fermez la porte de la cuisine," Ginger repeated.

"Qu'est-ce que c'est, mon amour, ma frou-frou?" called back Bill.

An electrician sitting in the fifth row had had enough.

"She said close the kitchen door," he said in abject disgust.

Ginger is so deadly serious that sometimes people think she has a wry sense of humor. She told the stage manager at Skowhegan, whose name was Bill, that he would have to have the crew call him something else for the week we were playing there as every time she heard someone shout out "Bill" she thought they were calling her husband and it made her very nervous.

"She's kidding, of course," the stage manager said to me, slightly dazed.

"She never kids," I said.

I suggested he might have the crew call him Sir Cedric Hard-wicke for the rest of the week. It would give us a little class, which we could certainly use.

I never knew how much Bill did on his own and how much Ginger put him up to. Ginger is a Christian Scientist and doesn't drink or smoke. Apparently Bill didn't either, but these seemed odd virtues for a roistering buddy of Errol Flynn's. I never really figured out whether Ginger wouldn't let him or whether these were virtues he affected to please her.

In any case, the virtues were not quite constant. He telephoned Guy Palmerton from a men's room on the road when he was driving Ginger from Chicago to Fitchburg and said:

"Don't let my wife know, but get me some booze, any kind of booze. I'm sure as hell going to need it by the time I get there."

I'm sure his life was no bed of roses. Of all the strong ladies I've known, Ginger was perhaps the strongest. And the most possessive. I was never sure whether Bill didn't talk to us or to anyone else backstage because he didn't want to or because she didn't want him to.

One night in the big tent at Storrowtown just outside Springfield, Massachusetts, Bill missed an entrance in a scene with Ginger. When he finally got on she played the scene with clenched teeth and she was so obviously upset that I sent the stage manager around to the side aisle where she would be making her exit.

"Who was he talking to?" Ginger demanded barely halfway up the aisle. "Tell me who he was talking to."

"He wasn't talking to anyone, Miss Rogers," the stage manager said. "They didn't have his props ready."

"Oh, the poor darling," Ginger said.

Bill missed another entrance in Nyack, New York, at a Wednesday matinee: he was out front in the audience counting the house. I never knew whether it was his idea or whether Ginger had sent him out to do it. But when the cue came for him to knock on the door in the third act there was no knock. Ginger and I looked apprehensively at each other, then we improvised a few lines. Not very bright. Mostly about the weather. And I did ask her about her cat, Pyewacket, and we talked about that for a while.

Suddenly we heard a gasp in the middle of the auditorium; then feet running toward the front door of the theater; then silence as Bill was presumably running down the alley toward the stage door; then the violent opening of the stage door; then feet running toward the stage. Then suddenly the footsteps stopped and it was a couple of more minutes before the knock finally came at the door. Why had the footsteps ceased? He had stopped at a mirror to comb his hairpiece.

About the only social gesture Ginger made on the whole tour was to invite the three supporting actors to her hotel suite in Dayton, Ohio, on the closing night of the tour. She served us hot dogs; there was one bottle of scotch; and there was a very ornate cake which had our names on it as follows: Ginger, Bill, Renie, Peter, and Mr. Kennedy.

There is something austere about the formality of Mr. Kennedy on a celebration cake. At least it said "and" Mr. Kennedy. It might have said "but."

Hopefully Ginger will find another husband. As it turned out, the last one apparently worked out worse for her than it did for me. But she must remember one thing. To paraphrase the popular Noël Coward song:

> *Don't put your husband on the stage, Ginger Rogers,*
> *Don't put your husband on the stage.*

STEVE ALLEN
AND JAYNE MEADOWS

JAYNE MEADOWS ALLEN is one of the few people in the theater who ever got me a job. I have had some substantial successes and some marvelous notices but I can safely say that in thirty-seven years no agent has ever gotten me a job. And very few other people. Almost anything I have ever done I have done on my own. I say this not out of ego but out of a kind of sad regret. Getting things on my own is a special talent I have developed out of necessity but it is a special talent that many fine actors do not have. And my greatest single regret about the theater is the number of first-rate talents I have seen and known who go through their whole lives never discovered and never given that one essential chance.

Robert Ryan gave me the plum job of my life, the Broadway revival of *The Front Page*. Arlene Francis demanded me for her production of *Janus*. Gloria Swanson demands me whatever she does. Jo Cotten gave me Maggie Sullavan, and Charlton Heston chose me for *A Man for All Seasons*. But that's about it. Except for Jayne Meadows.

I gave Jayne her first professional job and she never forgot it. Her name was Jayne Cotter then and her sister, now Audrey Meadows, was Audrey Cotter. The job I gave Jayne and for which she first got her Equity card was in a summer stock production of *The Man Who Came to Dinner* at the Trade School auditorium in Springfield, Massachusetts, and the leading lady was Kitty Carlisle, who had not yet met Moss Hart. The resident juvenile was Kevin McCarthy.

I had seen Jayne a number of times over the years and she always said, "We must do something together again." But nothing ever happened and you never really expect it to. She came backstage in Hollywood after the opening night of my Los Angeles production of *The Front Page*, glowing with enthusiasm, and said, "When are we going to do something together?"

"Any time," I said.

"Soon," she said.

I assumed that was the end of that, but she called me in New York a few months later and said that she and Steve had been asked to do a summer stock tour of Jean Kerr's play *Finishing Touches* and would I direct it. I said I would but was she sure they wanted to do that play.

"I don't think it's a very good play for the two of you," I said.

She asked me whether I had any other suggestions and off the top of my head I suggested that they do three of the one-act plays from Noël Coward's nine one-act play collection called *Tonight at 8:30*. She said they would buy all nine of them that day, that they would both read them, and call me back at midnight.

When the Allens say they will call you at midnight, you can plan your evening accordingly and the phone will ring at one minute to twelve. He is the most meticulous man I have ever met. He carries a tape recorder with him at all times, either hung around his neck or carried in his hand. In the middle of the most intimate conversation he will mumble down into his chest, "Get Harold the notes on so and so." It is unnerving at first, you feel that there is an unseen presence at the table, but ultimately it is very reassuring because you realize that at the very moment you are discussing a possible problem something is already being done about it. If you say something especially amusing or perceptive it is instantly recorded on the tape and filed away for future reference and possible use. He does not waste a single idea, which is probably why he comes up with so many good ones of his own.

They called at midnight; they had fallen in love with the Coward plays and they had decided which three they wanted to do.

When the Steve Allens, the Charlton Hestons, and the Robert Ryans decide to do a play in summer stock, money is of no importance. They want to be paid commensurate with their stature and they certainly want to be paid commensurate with what other stars are getting. But any one of them can make more money doing one "Movie of the Week" than they could possibly make on a ten-week summer tour. They do a play because they want to get back on the stage again, and since it is a labor of love they want everything right regardless of the expense.

For *Tonight at 8:30*, Jayne on her own engaged Edith Head to design her gowns for all three plays and they alone must have cost her more than her salary. While she was in London she took and paid for lessons in Cockney every day she was there. Steve put together with his orchestra a marvelous arrangement of appropriate songs to be played throughout the evening and at intermission. And none of the theaters was asked to share this expense.

They also took my advice and played what I call the "class" theaters on the summer circuit—the Cape Playhouse at Dennis, Massachusetts, the Ogunquit Playhouse in Ogunquit, Maine, and the fabulous old Elitch's Gardens Theater in

Denver—rather than playing the larger auditoriums and the tents where they could have made more money.

The tour was a great success. We sold out everywhere except in the shopping mall at Paramus, New Jersey, where, for whatever reason, we did not do as well. The notices were uniformly excellent.

Steve played the plays absolutely straight, which I had hoped he would. He was extremely touching in the serious one, *Still Life*, from which the movie *Brief Encounter* was made. Jayne was the great surprise to the audiences. Many of them apparently, even though they love her, think of her as a kind of scatterbrained flibbertigibbet, which indeed she is not. She gave three very distinctive, highly diversified, brilliant performances and though I know it may be sacrilege to say it I saw no reason to believe she wasn't every bit as good as Gertie Lawrence was.

We knew Steve's audience would expect him at some time in the evening to do one of his standup monologues. The only disagreement that he and I ever had was that I wanted him to do the monologue at the end of the evening and he wanted to do it at the very beginning before the curtain went up, which I really thought was wrong, as did all of the theater managers. But Steve was adamant and did it at the beginning, and initially it didn't work very well. But he is a bright man and he knew it wasn't working and he eventually devised a plan which made it work and satisfied even me. Instead of just going out and doing a straight standup routine he had a dressing table, mirrors, and makeup set on the stage. He would come out in front of the curtain, sit at the table, apply his makeup and put on his costume, meantime chatting with the audience. It gave a kind of continuity and theatricality that made the whole thing work.

The Allens are a marvelously happy couple, mutually devoted, and greatly complementary to each other. Like most comedians, he is unlike what his television fans would expect. He is a very quiet man, introspective, almost gloomy but not really

[87]

gloomy, just deadly serious. He is a fantastically busy man and really doesn't have time for chitchat. When he says something it is something he means and has thought about and it is usually perceptive and always sensible.

Jayne is all bubble and glitter and effervescence and if she just sits at your table at breakfast for a minute and shares a cup of coffee it starts your day with a lilt. They are both marvelously generous and I don't think the supporting members of the company were ever in the bar or the restaurant after the show, even if not actually with Steve and Jayne, that somehow mysteriously our checks weren't always picked up. Whenever we closed an engagement, anywhere, a few days later a gorgeous package would arrive from Saks or Bonwit's or Bloomingdale's with three especially selected very expensive sport shirts for me, obviously hand-picked by Jayne and with a handwritten note of thanks.

There is always some small thing about people that for some reason captures your attention. I wasn't as close to Steve as I was to Jayne, but there was one thing that made me feel very warm toward him. In addition to several children of Steve's by a previous marriage, of whom they are both very fond, they have a son of their own whom they adore. His name is Bill and he is a charming boy with the kind of instinctive good manners which seem to have gone out of fashion. In conversation Steve always refers to him as Bill, but when he is addressing him directly he always calls him "son." Kind of old-fashioned, I thought, and quite endearing.

I have a feeling that with all his frantic activities Steve has pressures which he would never admit to himself and certainly not to Jayne. But he also has a wonderful built-in release. He loves his music, he is brilliant at it, and it obviously relaxes him. When we were playing Elitch's Gardens, after the show every night he would sit at the piano with the combo at the Denver Continental and play for hours. He was rarely recognized, but one night I was sitting at the bar and a tourist sit-

ting next to me said in some surprise, "Isn't that Steve Allen?"
I said that it was.

"My God," he said, "what a shame to have him wind up in a
dump like this."

As I said before, Steve was very good about playing *Tonight
at 8:30* straight. No ad libs, though I am sure at times he was
tempted. He did get off one Steverino, though, in Paramus
when the occasion warranted it.

Jayne was sitting on the sofa in the first play in her
sequinned Edith Head dress. When she got up from the sofa a
black sequinned pillow which had been on the couch got up
with her and clung to her bejeweled behind as she crossed the
stage. The audience howled, but of course Jayne didn't know
why. When you hear an unexpected laugh on stage you always
assume someone's fly is open.

"Don't look now, darling," Steve said to her as she approached him, the pillow riding behind her like a gigantic bus-
tle, "but I think you're being followed."

WE CALL
EVERYBODY DARLING

TALLULAH BANKHEAD CALLED everybody "darling" for the same
reason that I do and that so many other theater people use the
word. It is not an affectation; it is sheer simple self-defense.
Many actors suffer from the same curse Tallulah had, and I
have, which is an excessive vagueness about names and faces,
and when we are extravagantly calling someone "darling" the
chances are pretty good that we haven't the least idea to whom
we are talking. It has nothing to do with how important someone is. If you have this particular curse you are apt not to recognize Garbo. In my particular case it has a lot to do with
being confronted out of context. In *The Front Page* with
twenty-four actors I knew the name of every single one when I
went to rehearsals where I was prepared for them; I doubt if I
would have known any one if I had met them in church or in a
supermarket. So if you don't know to whom you are talking,
"darling" is a marvelous compromise between affability and
anonymity.

We Call Everybody Darling

Gloria Swanson has no idea what anybody's name is. In every play we have done together she has always called the members of the supporting cast by the names of the characters they play in the play. She has had to give up gossiping entirely because she can't get the names right. She invariably has the basic facts but she gets the wrong people into the wrong beds and that creates considerable confusion.

When Gloria tells you a story about a major personality it is like playing "Twenty Questions" to figure out whom she is talking about. Some of it, of course, is easy. "Those two that always act together" is the Lunts.

"That Canadian girl with the bad side to her face" is Claudette Colbert. Though Gloria has no memory for names, she has an incredible recollection for unimportant details. She will refer to that big star at Metro who had the butler with the slight limp and the mole on his left cheek. This one is a little harder, but will probably wind up being Joan Crawford.

We had almost a dozen producers on the second Broadway production of *The Front Page* and Helen Hayes, who was in that version, could never tell one of them from the other. She referred to them as the "Twelve Apostles," but, as she said to me, "I never know which is Peter and which one is Paul."

Helen is not a "darling" type, so she referred to them simply as "Oh, hello." "Oh, hello, number one"; "Oh, hello, number two." "Darling" is really nicer.

Sardi's has been the scene of some of my greatest problems with not knowing to whom I was talking. It is not surprising, as anyone is apt to turn up there, and if you have this curse and in your mind you have safely pigeonholed someone in Beverly Hills and they have the bad taste to turn up at Sardi's unannounced, you are at a complete loss.

I walked into the Little Bar one night and was confronted by an extremely handsome and attractive man who greeted me effusively by name and ordered me a drink. I knew I knew him and I vaguely sensed that he was someone important but I couldn't figure out who. I felt sure it would come out during the conversation and I asked as many leading questions as I could.

"Are you still in the same place?"

"Oh, yes."

"What are you up to?"

"Oh, same old thing."

Not many clues there.

"Are you having dinner alone?" he asked. I said that I was and he promptly invited me to have dinner with him. We had each had a couple of martinis so I figured that during dinner he would surely have to go to the men's room and I could grab Vincent Sardi and find out who he was.

His bladder was as remarkable as his conversation. We talked interestingly about everything in the theater, every play in town, every performance, and finally got through the dessert and I figured I was never going to know. As he ordered a brandy he mumbled something about taking a leak and as his feet disappeared up the stairs I grabbed Vincent Sardi.

"Vincent, who am I sitting with?" I asked.

"You idiot," said Vincent. "That's Christopher Plummer."

Another night I was at the old long bar. It was just after curtain time and the bar was almost deserted. I was at the front end having an intense typical actor's conversation with a friend. I was making what seemed at the moment a point of monumental importance and I reached into my jacket pocket and took out a cigarette which I put into my mouth. A man standing at the opposite end of the bar walked down the whole length of the bar and lighted it. I was so involved in our conversation that it really seemed like an intrusion.

"Thank you," I said rather coldly and went back to making my point. The man just stayed there looking at me.

"I said, 'Thank you,'" I repeated sharply.

"Don't you remember me?" he asked.

"I certainly do not," I said.

"I'm Mark Robson. I produced your last picture."

"Well, that's probably why it will be my last picture," I said.

"It's like having the curse of the Hope diamond without the diamond."

Ruth Chatterton and I decided to engage Abe Feder to do the lighting for our touring production of Shaw's *Pygmalion*. We had neither one of us ever met him so Ruth invited him to her apartment at the Pierre and we spent a most pleasant two hours from five to seven, after which he left and I stayed for one more drink. I then went by myself to dinner at Sardi's. I was no more than seated when a man and a woman walked in. I had never seen the woman before but the man looked vaguely familiar and I knew I knew him. He came directly up to the table.

"Well, hello," he said.

"Hello," I said. Then, stalling for time, I added, "I haven't seen you in quite some time."

"No," he said. "Not since half an hour ago at Ruth Chatterton's."

At least being vague about names is better than getting them wrong. I remember coming out of the stage door in Chicago with Sylvia Sidney and Luther Adler, and two ladies waiting at the stage door pointed them out. "That's Sylvia Sidney," said one. "And that's her husband, Noodle Adler."

It's interesting in cases like this that the general public talks openly about celebrities directly in front of them almost as if they weren't actually there: as though they were watching them in a darkened movie theater or, over a six-pack of beer, on television at home. I think if Luther had spoken up and said, "My name is not Noodle Adler," the two ladies would have been just as startled as if he had spoken to them from the screen or right out of their TV tube. To the general public, celebrities aren't really real at all: they're just shadows on a screen, large or small.

What's a famous name anyway? I paid Bert Lahr $2,500 a week to do the play *Burlesque* for me in East Hartford, Connecticut, and one night during the rehearsal week he was to appear on a previously taped talk show. We took time out from rehearsals and went over to the local bar to watch the show. The minute Bert appeared, the bartender said, "Oh, there's what's-his-name."

Then there's the case of the new face: it can also get you into trouble. Shirley Eder, the effervescent and omnipresent columnist from Detroit, who is an old friend, buzzed over to my table in Sardi's where I was sitting with a friend one day and said:

"Darling, have you lost your mind? What was that terrible play about a circus you sent to Barbara Stanwyck? She sent it to me and neither one of us understood a word of it. It was awful."

She then turned laughingly to my friend in an effort to include him in the conversation.

"I hope you didn't write it," she said.

"As a matter of fact, I did," he said.

And he had.

I had never before seen Shirley at a loss for words.

And of course, there are the television actors. People know the face and the name of the character the actor plays but rarely the actor's own name. I'm sure there are lots of people who know the real names of Starsky and Hutch, but I'm sure there are lots more like myself who don't.

I took John Travolta out on a tour of *Bus Stop* two summers ago and he broke a seventy-six-year attendance record at the Lakewood Theatre in Skowhegan, Maine, but only because they stressed that he was "Barbarino" on the TV show "Welcome Back, Kotter." John Travolta as John Travolta two summers ago wouldn't have sold a ticket. It's quite a different story now that he is the hottest new young star in films.

I remember Vivian Vance telling me at the peak of the success of "I Love Lucy" that she would never do another series unless she was able to use at least her own first name. "Thanks to 'Lucy,'" Vivian said, "I'm one of the best-known women in the country. But I'm known by the wrong name. Everybody calls me Ethel Mertz."

It was interesting that when the spinoffs came for the other "Lucy" series she apparently stuck to her word, because from that time on in every show the character she played was also called Vivian.

That is why the biggest names in television and the biggest draws in summer stock are the people on the game and panel shows who use their own names and get a million dollars' worth of publicity every time they use them. You don't have to explain who Johnny Carson is. Or Steve Allen. Or Arlene Francis.

Another problem with names in our business is that we are not always supposed to be ourselves. Sometimes we are quite conspicuously supposed to be somebody else. Cesar Romero got mixed up about that once and completely fouled up the denouement of a play I had written called *The Seven Deadly Arts* on its opening night in Paramus, New Jersey. The third act had built to a scene of enormous tension, the stage was full of people, and they were all waiting for an urgent phone call. The phone finally rang. Cesar was supposed to rush to it, pick it up, and say in a voice of supreme authority, "This is Frederick Symington III." Where Cesar's mind was, I don't know, but he picked up the phone and said with supreme authority, "This is Cesar Romero." The audience loved it, but it wasn't much help in unraveling the plot.

Katharine Hepburn's mother invited Gloria Swanson and me to the Hepburn family manse at Fenwick on the Connecticut side of the Sound when Gloria and I were playing *A Goose for the Gander* at Ivoryton.

Kate Hepburn herself had called from California and suggested the invitation, thinking that we might enjoy the house, which was gorgeous and right on the water. We also enjoyed the whole family, most of whom were like minor carbons of Kate and all of whom spoke in a kind of native Hepburn patois which made us vaguely wish we had brought an interpreter. We particularly enjoyed Mrs. Hepburn, who was every inch the matriarch and a perfect hostess, except that she too apparently had inherited the theatrical curse.

As we walked through the door Mrs. Hepburn fell upon Gloria and said:

"My dear, before you sit down, before I even offer you a drink, you have got to let me introduce my cook. She's been in seventh heaven ever since she knew you were coming and she has prepared some marvelous things for us, but I promised I would let her meet you the minute you walked through the door."

Gloria was not displeased with such adulation and graciously agreed.

"Della, Della," called Mrs. Hepburn and Della materialized instantly from behind a door where she had obviously been listening.

"Here she is, Della," crowed Mrs. Hepburn, "here she is. Della, this is Miss Cornell."

I played Ivoryton again recently with Miss Hepburn's niece, Katharine Houghton, in *Sabrina Fair* and the whole Hepburn family turned out. After the play, Kate's brother, Richard, told me that the Swanson-Cornell story has been a family favorite for years.

There was a chairwoman of a famous woman's club in Chicago who I thought had really come up with the ideal solution to the problems of names and identifications. Orson Welles, Maurice Evans, and I were guests of honor at her club on their annual "Distinguished Guests" day and as chairwoman she carried with her at all times a tiny metal file, carefully indexed with all sorts of typewritten cards in it. You felt that no matter who might turn up, she could instantly open the file, leaf through the index, pull out a card and tell you anything and everything about them. Obviously Orson, Maurice, and I were all carefully tucked away in the file.

We weren't an ideal combination of guests. Orson and Maurice weren't too fond of each other. They were always in conflict and in competition; and on this particular occasion nei-

Steve Allen and Jayne Meadows playing three widely different roles in separate one-act plays that make up Tonight at 8:30. *Above left,* Hands Across the Sea, *above right,* Still Life, *and below,* Fumed Oak. *(Photos by Bill Allen).*

Ruth Chatterton in the touring production of Shaw's Pygmalion.

Linda Fields and Cesar Romero in the Skowhegan, Maine, production of Strictly Dis-honorable.

Vincent Price and Jane Wyatt in the Los Angeles production of The Winslow Boy, *1950. (Photo by Wilson Millar)*

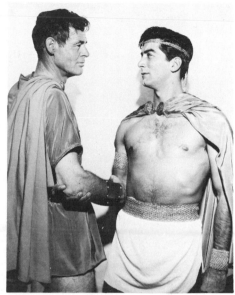

Robert Ryan and Ray Danton in the Hollywood production of Tiger at the Gates. (Photo by Wilson Millar)

John Ireland in the Hollywood production of Tiger at the Gates. (Photo by Wilson Millar)

June Allyson and Harold J. Kennedy in a scene from the twenty-week tour of Goodbye Ghost.
(Photo by David Mobley)

Charlton Heston in the Chicago production of A Man for All Seasons. (Photo by Lydia C. Heston)

Charlton Heston in rehearsal for A Man for All Seasons (Photo by Lydia C. Heston)

The unfinished theater where A Man for All Seasons *was eventually staged. (Photos by Lydia C. Heston)*

ther one of their shows was doing good business in Chicago. We were playing the road company of *Julius Caesar* at the Erlanger and directly across the backstage alley Maurice Evans was doing his production of *Henry IV*. Down the street there was a production of George Abbott's *Room Service* whose wicked press agent had taken out newspaper ads saying "Positively NOT Shakespeare," and they were selling out. Maurice Evans of course was in his own production but Orson had just flown in from New York to try to hype our business. We had timed his visit to coincide with the "Distinguished Guests" luncheon.

The luncheon was typical. Hundreds of ladies in huge hats. Tepid chicken à la king on cold toast; tiny hard green peas, a bedraggled clump of lettuce that tasted as though it had been seasoned with dishwater, and a tiny mound of orange sherbet.

When all of that was over it was time to introduce the distinguished guests. There were about eight of us sitting at a long table on the dais. Orson at one end, Maurice Evans at the other; the chairwoman center; me for some strange reason next to her; and on the other side of me a lady who was like a delicate porcelain prototype of Billie Burke.

The chairlady rose, clanked on her water glass, and took out her little metal file.

"I would like to introduce first by far our most distinguished guest," she said. "Mr. Maurice Evans."

Maurice beamed. Orson frowned his famous frown. The lady filed quickly through to the E's and pulled a typewritten card from which she began to read.

"Mr. Evans is playing a small part in Orson Welles's production of *Julius Caesar*," she started.

There were gasps and cries of "No, no," and the poor lady stopped, confused.

There is one thing to be said of an efficient filing system. If it's wrong, it's wrong, and what do you do?

"Mr. Evans is . . ." the lady stammered and looked helplessly back at the file. "Mr. Evans is . . ."

[97]

And then finally it was all too much for her.

"I'm sure I don't know who Mr. Evans is," she said and sat down.

"Billie Burke" on the other side of me immediately leaped to her feet and she was going to save the day.

She rapped for attention. "If Mildred weren't so exhausted," she told the members, "from arranging this lovely luncheon—(pause for applause)—and she is exhausted, but it was worth it, wasn't it?—(more applause)—if she weren't so exhausted she would know, as every one of us knows, who Maurice Evans is. He is the greatest English-speaking actor in the world today. His is a face that is known in every home in America—and in England too—and it is my pleasure and privilege to present to you now the immortal star of *Henry the Fourth*—Mister Maurice Evans."

With which, on a note of triumph, she crossed, pulled me out of my chair, and dragged me to the center of the platform.

When I recovered myself, which wasn't easy, I said, "Well, at least part of the introduction is right. I am playing a small part in Orson Welles's production of *Julius Caesar*. But I am not Maurice Evans. And obviously Orson Welles does not pay my salary to run around introducing Maurice Evans. I came here to talk about *Julius Caesar*. And that's what I'm going to talk about."

So I talked about *Julius Caesar* and when I finished there wasn't one single hand clap. There was what you might call a standing ovation. To the extent that all the ladies were on their feet and in full flight toward the doors. The entire banquet hall was cleared, I think, in a minute and three quarters. Orson and Maurice were never introduced. They were left sitting gloomily alone at the head table and as far as I know there has never been another "Distinguished Guests" gathering at this particular club.

Of course, if you have a famous face you can usually be sure of a welcome no matter what you are doing. When Cesar Romero was playing *Strictly Dishonorable* for me at Skowhegan, Maine, he inadvertently drove his rented car the wrong way down a one-way street. A car coming in the opposite direction jammed on its brakes; an irate woman lowered the window and shouted:

"You stupid jerk, you're on a one way str— Oh, hello, how lovely to see you."

A potential backer for one of our plays, whom we had never met, invited Gloria Swanson and me to a cocktail party at his Park Avenue apartment. We went and had been there an hour and a half before we discovered we were in the wrong apartment and at the wrong party. It all happened quite naturally. The doorman gave us the wrong apartment number; we rang the bell; the hostess, though presumably surprised, was delighted that Gloria Swanson was coming to her party. She said, "Miss Swanson, how lovely to see you," and Gloria said, "And this is Mr. Kennedy," and we were introduced to everyone on a wave of popularity. It wasn't until some time later when I began to seek out the host to discuss business that I found out that we were on the fourteenth floor—the party to which we had been invited was on the seventeenth. We subsequently got to the right one but the first one was really more fun.

Arlene Francis knows my name but she always calls me "Bull," which is short for Bull Montana, who was the symbol of balls in silent movies before the sound track allowed us to hear them rattle. The nickname came and has stuck as a result of a remark I made to Arlene when we were having a very serious discussion about the function of a director. I was saying that I thought it was the director's obligation to tell an actor everything, no matter how personal, if it might be important to the play and the performance. Obviously if it is highly personal you don't discuss it in rehearsal or in front of the other actors, but you take someone to lunch and talk about it privately. I was saying that I had done it most successfully with Vincent Price, who is an old friend, and who was appearing for me in a

[99]

Los Angeles revival of *The Winslow Boy*. Now, Vincent is one of the great camps of the world, and genuinely amusing. He has made a huge success camping his way through all those horror films, but that wasn't what I wanted in *The Winslow Boy*. I explained to Vincent that I thought it was an extraordinarily beautiful play and a beautiful part and that I thought he ought to play it absolutely straight down the line without an extraneous gesture or an added raise of the eyebrow. He agreed with me completely and urged me to watch him carefully throughout rehearsals and cut out anything at all that I found excessive.

It was extremely rewarding when the notices came out. Almost every critic to a man echoed the Los Angeles *Times*, which wrote: "Mr. Price has seen fit to tone down some of his annoying movie mannerisms and become once again the brilliant straightforward actor he was in *Angel Street* and *Victoria Regina*."

All, as I pointed out to Arlene, because I warned him not to camp.

Then I added, "Now, mind you, dear, I'm not exactly Bull Montana."

She roared and the name has stuck to me ever since.

Speaking of names, how would you like to have Cary Grant in a play and not be able to say he was in it? That frightening proposition was half-tentatively, half-jokingly offered to me by Mr. Grant himself over the telephone, about ten years ago. I had written him a letter about the possibility of his doing some summer stock. It didn't seem likely he would consider it but I write to everybody and sometimes I get some surprising responses.

One year I neglected to write to James Mason and he spent three days trying to track me down across the country because that was the year he decided he wanted to act in summer stock. And he did, co-starring with his then wife, Pamela, and his daughter Portland in Viña Delmar's *Midsummer*, in which they were all very good.

In any case, Cary Grant phoned in answer to my letter. When that voice said, "Mr. Kennedy, this is Cary Grant," there was no mistaking it. Some voices are unique beyond all belief.

It is like Peggy Cass, who was unexpectedly passing through the town where Gary Moore has his summer home, calling Gary and saying, "Guess who this is."

"With that voice," said Gary, "who else could it be?"

After the amenities were exchanged Cary Grant explained that he was really just picking my brains, that he was curious about many aspects of summer stock, and that actually he would like to play a week or two but that he would only play, if at all, under circumstances which would be of no use to me.

"What I would really like to do," he said, "is go to a very small theater up in Maine and work under an assumed name. Just to have the fun of doing a part in a play. But I am certainly not prepared for the rat race I would get into if I played a part under my own name."

"And I wouldn't let you use Archie Leach, either," he added quickly, reading my mind.

He quickly conceded his whole idea was useless because even if some manager guaranteed not to advertise him, the smaller the town, the sooner word would get around that Cary Grant was there. He did say, and I know this to be true, that he felt there were many big stars in Hollywood who would really love to do a play and even summer stock, and who genuinely didn't care about the big monetary difference, but who simply didn't want to lay their careers that firmly on the line. The critics are not notoriously kind to Hollywood people and the bigger they are, the greater the target.

We talked for about half an hour and he wished me well. It would have been nice to have tried it. How would you have liked to go slumming to some tiny barn theater in New Hampshire and find, when you got in, that the local resident leading man was Cary Grant?

To wind up the subject of names, I suppose my worst personal experience was when I returned to my hometown of Holyoke, Massachusetts, to open a new theater in an amusement park there. I was directing and playing with Cesar Romero in *Strictly Dishonorable*. Cesar and I had arrived in Holyoke at midnight the night before. We had a morning rehearsal at the Masonic Temple right next door to the telephone company on Maple Street.

When we took our lunch break, Cesar and I headed for the local luncheonette and had to pass the phone company offices. As we passed, windows flew open and heads appeared as all the switchboard girls recognized Cesar, and oohed and aahed and called out to him.

I was more interested in a sandwich and was forging on ahead when a man came out of the main entrance and shouted, "Harold! Harold!"

I waved to him.

"Hello, hello, darling," I said and continued on.

Cesar caught me by the arm.

"Isn't that your brother?" he asked.

"Oh, my God," I said. "Hello. Hello, DARLING."

QUEEN HELEN

UNLIKE GINGER ROGERS, who never smiles, Helen Hayes is tired of smiling. The dual crown of Victoria and First Lady sits uneasily on her head.

"I didn't ask to be Queen," Helen says rather wistfully, and I think all the genuflecting and royal treatment bore her to death. She doesn't want to be the White Sister or Julie Haydon or a national monument. She's a feisty, gutsy, Irish biddy with a wicked sense of humor and a will of her own.

People who know only the royal Helen have always wondered about her supposedly perfect marriage to Charlie MacArthur. If you know the real Helen you will agree with her that it was probably the mating of the century.

Of course, Charlie MacArthur was one of the sharp wits of all time, in the theater and out of it. I think my favorite put-down of Charlie's, and he was a master at it, was his devastation of a critic of somewhat dubious sexual persuasion on a now defunct afternoon paper. The critic not only severely panned Ben Hecht and Charlie's play, *Ladies and Gentlemen,* but also dragged Helen into it. Charlie had written it, his part of it anyway, especially for Helen, and the critic ended his review by saying, "As for Miss Hayes, the trouble with her is that she has been seeing too much of Charlie MacArthur."

"What are you going to do to that sonofabitch?" demanded Charlie's cronies at 21 the next day.

"I've already taken care of him," said Charlie calmly. "I have sent him a poisoned choirboy."

The opening of the original *Front Page* was the night Helen and Charlie became engaged and Helen was full of memories of that night when we flew her East from Hollywood, where she was filming *Airport,* to be guest of honor at our opening. The first opening of our revival on Broadway was in May 1969 and at that time Helen was not a member of the cast; she later joined at her own request when we reopened in September.

As a member of our opening night audience she told the New York *Times* she knew there was nothing to worry about after the boys in Chicago's criminal court press room got their first laugh some ten seconds after the curtain went up.

"Charlie and Ben would have loved it," she told the *Times.* "It ranked with the original production."

At the party after the opening she told Sid Zion the story of the original opening night.

"I was far more nervous when *The Front Page* opened in the summer of 1928. I was in *Coquette* at the time and I knew Charlie wouldn't marry me unless he had a hit. Jed Harris, who produced both shows, closed *Coquette* for the night so I could see *The Front Page.*

"I sat in the balcony so I could be near the boys who insisted on sitting out on the fire escape. When I knew it was going to be okay during the first act I ran out and jumped into Charlie's arms and started babbling about the great reaction. Charlie held me tight and then held me off and asked me if I'd marry him. And I said, 'You took the words right out of my mouth.'"

[104]

They were married three days later.

Our revival of *The Front Page* was only supposed to run for four weeks but the notices were such raves that it was immediately extended an additional four and could easily have run all summer, but the management got cold feet when the advance for the summer months wasn't as strong as they felt it should be and when Bob Ryan, who after all had only committed himself to a four-week run, said that he would continue all summer only if he could have Monday nights off to spend with his family in New Hampshire. So they closed the play on the Fourth of July week when it was still doing big business and that was when the new group that Helen called "The Twelve Apostles" came in and urged me to reopen the show in September, which we did. That was when Helen joined the cast in the role of Mrs. Grant, which she says was modeled after her own mother, who slightly disapproved of Charlie just as Mrs. Grant disapproves of Hildy Johnson in the play.

I was inadvertently almost responsible for keeping Helen out of our production. One of the new investor-producers was a dress designer with a home in Westport; Peggy Cass had immediately labeled him "The Stitch Queen." He called me in great excitement one day, and after I finally figured out who he was, he reported with glee that Helen Hayes had been at his house for cocktails and that she had said she wanted to be in the cast of the play.

Nothing bores me more in the theater than cocktail talk. It is always a waste of everybody's time. The late Joan Crawford would sit at a cocktail party and swear it was her heart's desire to do a stage play. If you took her seriously and followed up with a firm and sensible offer you would get an equally firm letter, written on a more rational basis, saying that she had no intention of doing a play ever, at any time, under any circumstances. I think the only thing agents are any good for is extricating their clients from the rash promises the clients make at cocktail parties.

So I said to the Stitch Queen, "Listen, why don't you social-ites up there in Westport just drink your martinis and mind your business, and leave the casting up to the professionals."

There always has to be that one time you guess wrong. A few days later the Chief Apostle called me and said, "Harold, Helen Hayes is very upset. She thinks you don't want her in the play."

I called Helen immediately. "Is this for real?" I asked her. "Would you really consider playing that part?"

"It's such a marvelous production," she said. "And reopening a play is always a little risky. I thought maybe if I joined the cast it might give you just a little extra shot of interest."

Indeed it did, enough so that we ran from September through March the second time around.

I must say I had some qualms about directing the First Lady in a small part in her husband's play. As a long time Hayes fan, I was keenly aware of the acting legend and I was also aware that she must have seen many performances of *The Front Page* all over the world. So I was afraid I might have a star arriving at rehearsal not only with a star's preconceived ideas but with the rather firmer ideas of the author's widow.

Authors' widows are savagely protective of their husbands' brainchildren. I did over eight hundred performances of Moss Hart's play *Light Up the Sky* with his widow, the lovely Kitty Carlisle Hart. As an actress, and she's a good one, she will take graciously and gratefully any suggestion you make. But no sug-gestions about Moss's play. Not a word cut. And she is right. In the same way, Rose Hecht, Ben's widow, refused to release the television rights to *The Front Page* unless she was guaranteed that I would have complete and total say on the editing of the script.

Not so Helen in rehearsals. She brings to the director no preconceived ideas. Just lays before you a vast treasurehouse of talent and lets you select the best or most suitable. Early in re-hearsal she said to me what she had said to a previous director, "Don't direct me, edit me." And that was all that was needed.

An embittered unemployed actor accosted me at the bar at Sardi's during the run of *The Front Page* and said, "Now don't tell me you direct Helen Hayes." I said, "It's very simple. Miss Hayes does every single thing I ask her to do. The only difference is that she does it about two hundred times better than anyone else could."

The Catholic Actors' Guild honored Helen as Woman of the Year on November 9, 1974, and they asked me for a quote for their souvenir program. This is the quote I gave them:

"Helen Hayes is to a theatrical director what the gift of a flawless instrument must be to a practicing musician. Just play softly on it and out comes the most beautiful music in the world."

I think Helen's neatest acting trick in *The Front Page* was to disappear, on demand, into the scenery. I had explained to her that since she was playing a relatively minor role there were certain times when I really didn't want the audience looking at her, which is very difficult with a major star. "Oh, fine," said Helen and somehow she became totally invisible, although she was right there on that stage. But when the time came that we wanted the audience to watch her, those ten million candles lighted up behind the eyes.

Helen has a wonderful awareness of her unique position. She also has a sense of humor about it. She told me one night in her dressing room about a young actress who had been fired from one of the productions at the APA in which Helen was starring. Helen tried to console the girl.

"I'm no better at this stage of rehearsal than you are," Helen told her. "But they wouldn't dare fire me. It would be like spitting on the American flag."

But whether she likes it or not, after all those years of identification she does wear the badge of royalty unmistakably upon her. I remember when her daughter, Mary MacArthur, who was a dear friend, was alive, we used to play "the game" at Mary's apartment and Helen would frequently join in. "The game" is the old game of "indications," where two teams act out in pantomime various play titles or quotations and race to see which team can guess correctly first. Helen was certainly the best actress, but she was the lousiest game player. The royal aura around her intimidated all her fellow players and no matter what she was acting out her team would guess Victoria, or Queen Elizabeth, or at least Marie of Romania. If Helen pantomimed holding a mop, the other players were sure she was holding a scepter.

Kitty Carlisle often recalls one of the saddest moments she and Moss Hart shared together. They stood together at the rear of a packed theater in Olney, Maryland, watching Helen give a brilliant performance of a light play called *Good Housekeeping*. They knew what Helen onstage did not know, that the producer was waiting in the wings with a car outside to rush Helen to New York: word had just come that her beloved Mary was dying.

The story I like best that Helen told me, and I remember roaring with laughter in the dressing room at the way she told it, was her description of a highly embarrassing encounter with another first lady of the theater at high noon in what Helen described as a "posh" Beverly Hills restaurant.

I will not use the other lady's name, as it is a private story and I'm sure Helen would not want me to. Anyway, the other is a lovely lady, a major stage star, a Tony winner, warm and darling, and as Irish as they come. But like the rest of us Irish she is not reluctant to bend an elbow. However, like Tallulah she never does it when she's working, and also like Tallulah and most of the Irish, she never becomes hostile or belligerent when she is drinking. She is ebullient and effusive enough anyway, and with a few drinks, love and exuberance just ooze out of her. We will call her Miriam.

Helen had a day off from the filming of *Airport* and she was being very much plain Mrs. Charles MacArthur and entertaining two of Charlie's maiden aunts from Pasadena at this posh restaurant in Beverly Hills. I gather from Helen that the

rest of the MacArthur family is, to put it mildly, considerably
more conservative than Charlie and they were having a very elegant, proper, Pasadena-type luncheon. Helen Hokinson hats
firmly on the heads. Every hair carefully in place. One daiquiri
each. Not too strong. A nice salad. And a lovely mousse. And
tea. Lots of tea. And quiet, genteel conversation. No shop talk.
Just three conservative, elderly ladies who might well be on
their way to a matinee of *Smilin' Through* or *Peg o' My Heart.*
As luncheon was winding up, Helen became aware of a voice
that was getting louder and louder in the next booth. The
booths were very high and you couldn't see who was in them,
but there was no mistaking the voice. It was Miriam and the
elbow was obviously very well bent. Helen's heart stopped and
she looked at her two companions.

"I love Miriam," Helen said to me, "and I wouldn't mind if
I were alone. But those two ladies would never have been able
to deal with it. And I would never have been able to explain it.

"So I waved frantically for a waiter. I didn't dare speak for
fear Miriam would hear me. I whispered for the check. I
abruptly thrust at the two ladies their pocketbooks and their
packages and their shopping bags. 'I have to leave this minute,'
I whispered, and, pushing the two of them in front of me, I
started to tiptoe across what must have been the dance floor at
night."

The three of them got just to the center of the floor when
Miriam saw them.

"Helen," she screamed. "Helen," she bellowed and started
toward them. Helen says Miriam is noted for being easily audible on any stage in the country, including municipal auditoriums and outdoor ball parks, and she could certainly be heard
in that restaurant. Everybody looked up from lunch.

"Helen," Miriam shouted as she charged toward her. "I love
you. If you were a man I'd fuck you."

With which big Miriam threw both arms around little Helen
and they toppled together to the floor while all of Hollywood
looked on.

"I could just see what they were thinking," Helen said. "The two first ladies of the theater, groveling on the floor at high noon. And they talk about Hollywood."

The only problem we had with Helen on *The Front Page* was what to do about her curtain call. Curtain calls in the theater are as important to the actors as billing and they go in reverse order. For instance, if you have the first star billing you get the last star curtain call, which is the most important. Helen was determined that Bob Ryan should have the final call which, with the importance of the part, he was certainly entitled to. She also felt that Peggy Cass and Bert Convy, because of their parts, should have later and more important calls. But Peggy nearly had a fit. "You think I'm going to take a curtain call after Helen Hayes," she wailed. "They'd throw rocks at me."

It was eventually worked out, as most things were with *The Front Page*, in a rather charming manner. We took all the curtain calls without Helen. Then Bob Ryan took his bow and we all joined hands and the whole company bowed together. Then Bob held up his hand to the audience and walked up to the center door and led Helen by the hand onstage. So the first lady and, in my opinion, the first gentleman of the theater, shared the final call together.

JOHN IRELAND AND HOW NOT TO LEARN YOUR LINES

JOHN IRELAND IS one of those actors who will not learn lines by himself. John wants to be cued from the first minute he picks up the script. Cueing is something you should do for an actor only after he has committed the lines to memory. Then you sit down with the script, fire the cue lines at him, and he repeats his own lines over and over again until they are so securely implanted in his mind that he can say them while he is mixing a drink, punching someone in the nose, engaging in swordplay, or whatever extra demands the play may make of him.

John and I have a standard greeting whenever we meet. It is, "Hello, Kimo, you back?" This was (approximately) the first line of a play called *Petticoat Fever*, which John and his then wife, Joanne Dru, did for me in summer stock and it was the only line John ever really knew. We would start rehearsals and John would come on like Gangbusters and say, "Hello, Kimo, you back?" then reach for the script and read the rest of the play.

He is a darling man and a dear friend and I eventually realized that the only way he would ever get his lines in a new play was if I spoon-fed them to him. So when he was going to do *Tiger at the Gates* for me in Hollywood with an impressive cast including Robert Ryan, Mary Astor, Marilyn Erskine, and Ray Danton, I moved in with him at a motel on the Sunset Strip and began the laborious process of feeding him the lines.

We had a kind of pact that we would not go out for drinks or dinner any day until at least twenty pages of the script had been memorized. Things were going relatively well until one afternoon about five o'clock, when the phone rang. I answered it as I always did, being somewhat like the keeper of an alcoholic ward. The voice on the other end asked for John and said, "This is (a celebrated Hollywood star)."

"John," I said, "It's _____."

"I don't know her."

"Nevertheless," I said and handed him the phone.

The lady was known in Hollywood for her favorite color, having a passionate predilection for it. It was rumored that her entire house was decorated in it; certainly her dressing room at the studio was; and for a time she even tinted her blond hair that hue.

There was a momentary pause after John picked up the phone and then he said, "Well, I guess it's true."

After a little more perfunctory conversation John hung up and said to me, "I'm going out."

"What did she say that you answered, 'I guess it's true'?" I asked him.

He blushed deeply.

Well, if that's what she asked him, it was indeed true and was well known in all Hollywood.

He picked up his jacket and started out the door.

"Why don't you take this with you?" I said, holding out the script.

"What would I do with that?"

"You might read it just for openers," I suggested.

[112]

He disappeared and was gone for three days. When he came back I don't know what condition he was in, but the script was still virgin.

Anyway, when we got back to town from a tryout in Phoenix, his dressing room at the theater had been repainted and redecorated in the lady's favorite color.

JUNE BUG

How DO I DESCRIBE June Allyson, the darling of the forties and the fifties, the perennial dream of "the girl next door," the prize every red-blooded American boy wanted to take to the graduation prom? Let June describe herself as she did to me in the bar of our hotel in Nyack where we were playing a play I had written called *Goodbye Ghost* with which we toured the country for more than twenty weeks.

"I'm June Bug, I'm Junie Poo, I'm Cutie Junie, but, baby, don't ever turn your back."

A harsh description and not a true one. She's basically a darling, loving cuddly lady, but she has moments of insecurity, as all those ladies from Metro had.

The strong ladies—the Tallulahs, the Swansons, the Ina Claires—are very easy to deal with. They know exactly what they want and it doesn't change from minute to minute or even from year to year. They are not interested in extraneous opinions. But a star like June, out of her own insecurity, will not only listen to but actually seek advice from people who are spectacularly ill-equipped to give it.

June also had a husband. I say had, because she married him twice and divorced him twice, but he was much in evidence at the time. I have nothing against husbands per se. Lynn Fontanne had a husband and I would have been delighted to have him around. But his name happened to be Alfred Lunt. An extraneous husband around the theater is a nuisance. An extraneous anything is a nuisance. The trouble with extraneous people around a theatrical production—husbands, lovers, family—is that they feel lost without a function and the only way they can create a function for themselves is to manufacture problems and then become heroes by helping to solve those very same problems. The trouble with that is that the problems create more chaos than the ultimate happy solution is worth.

June's husband had been Dick Powell's barber. There's certainly nothing wrong with being a barber. I've enough respect for barbers that I would not dream of walking into one of their shops, picking up a scissors, and starting to cut their customers' hair. In the same way I would prefer that a barber not walk into my rehearsal and start directing the play. Better he should take care of her hair.

June herself is the first to admit she's hardly a fashion plate and she loves to tell the story about what Esther Williams said to her when they were both working at Metro. They were together in the wardrobe department at the same time and Esther was being fitted to a gorgeous, form-clinging, gold lamé dress and June was positively drooling with envy.

"Oh, Esther," she said, "I wish I could wear something like that."

"You never can, honey," Esther said. "They don't make them with Peter Pan collars."

June's husband was named A. Glenn Maxwell. He walked up to Frank Sinatra, whom he had never met, when we were playing *Goodbye Ghost* in Miami and said:

"I'm A. Glenn Maxwell."

"What," asked Frank, "is a Glenn Maxwell?"

Glenn was a sweet man and I liked him, but he was in an area where he didn't belong and he was trying to find a place for himself where there was no place. Unlike Ginger Rogers' husband, who wanted to act, Glenn wanted to direct, and he had never directed a play before. I put his name on the program as director on the last summer tour, but since I had already directed the play and we had the same cast, it meant nothing.

It is hard to say how much Glenn contributed to June's insecurities and how much indeed he may actually have helped her.

There must have been something rotten in the early state of Metro-Goldwyn-Mayer. All the ladies from that era—the Judy Garlands, the Gloria DeHavens, the Junes—have an absolute phobia about any kind of discipline or authority. They shy violently away from it like frightened animals who have been harnessed and been hurt by the harnessing. I don't mean a Prussian discipline like Otto Preminger's. I mean a simple basic requirement such as "Rehearsal will be at eleven o'clock." They don't want to rehearse at eleven o'clock. Or twelve. Or one. Or any specific time. And you can bet whatever hour rehearsal is, these ladies will come late. They will always have a bona fide excuse. They are delayed at the costumer's or the wigmaker's, or they are making a publicity pitch; but obviously if one wanted to be punctual at rehearsal these appointments could have been made at another time. These are not evil ladies and they are certainly not untalented, but it is a pattern they all have and it undoubtedly goes back to a stage in their early training which they still resent and are still fighting. They are all obviously still frightened by the ghost of Louis B. Mayer.

These ladies, and indeed most of Hollywood's biggest stars, uniformly seem to find their closest friend and confidante in their hairdresser. Or their makeup artist. Or their stand-in. I am not referring to the obvious case of a Barbra Streisand; I mean they seem to seek a companion who has no authority over them.

June had been in the chorus of a couple of Broadway musicals but had not been on the stage at all since becoming a big star. In 1965, however, the Paper Mill Playhouse in Milburn, New Jersey, had persuaded her to make her legitimate stage debut in the play *Janus*, directed by Alfred de Liagre, Jr., who had produced the original Broadway show with Margaret Sullavan. Scott McKay and Murray Matheson were playing the two male leads and I was playing a rich character part that I had previously played with Arlene Francis and for which Arlene had recommended me.

I was never closer to June than I was when we first met. I was merely an actor in the company and had no other function and she was able to relate to me solely as a fellow actor and a friend. I in turn required nothing of her.

June was extremely nervous and she was by no means secure in her lines. She clung to me for encouragement and support and we became friends very quickly. Since I had done the play before, I was able to reassure her about it and as the week went on she really didn't want me out of her sight. But also as the week went on she became more and more nervous and on Saturday morning, with the opening on Tuesday, she had to leave the rehearsal at least seven or eight times and be ill in the ladies' room.

De Liagre finally dismissed rehearsal but asked the cast to remain available, and later in the day Glenn called and said June was ready to work. We all went up to her suite in the Regency and sat around and read the lines. June was much more relaxed and comfortable in the informal atmosphere of the suite and I was very encouraged.

The management was terrified that she would never open, but I thought she would and she did. And she was very good, too. But the insecurity was there. When the curtain fell and I kissed her and congratulated her she said, "I am convinced I am a total and absolute failure in this play."

She believed it. And the sad thing was that it wasn't true.

The next day was Wednesday, a matinee day, and I went to her dressing room before the performance and said, "Now you've had the baby. It's all gravy from now on. Relax and have fun with it."

But she was more nervous during the matinee than she had been opening night. Often that happens in the theater. Sheer nerves can frequently carry you through an opening night. June told me that Wednesday afternoon she couldn't remember anything at all about the opening on the preceding night.

On the second performance of a play the cold reality begins to set in and the nerves are different and sometimes worse. That's why second nights in the theater are notoriously let-downs.

We got through the matinee well enough and June was going to lie down between shows. I went out for dinner and when I came back the stage doorman said Miss Allyson wanted to see me. I went to her dressing room and she was lying on the couch, groaning in pain. Glenn had gone to call an ambulance. She asked me to hold her until he got back and I did. There was no question that she was ill. Whether she had made herself ill is beside the point. We can have a heart attack out of fright as well as any other way. And she was a very sick girl.

The ambulance arrived before the curtain of the play and the performance was canceled. I called the hospital around midnight from New York and was told that June was under sedation. When I called the next afternoon I was told that she and Glenn had flown back to Hollywood.

I think the management at the Paper Mill always felt that she should have stayed in the New Jersey hospital in the hope that she might have been well enough in a few days to continue with the play. And they are probably right.

But she was a very frightened lady and I think she wanted to get home. Her answer to fright is the same as mine has always been, and as that of many people is—flight. And I understood it.

There were no performances at Paper Mill the rest of that week, which, of course, was a substantial loss for the management, and the following week Imogene Coca, who had played the part before, came in and finished the last two weeks of the engagement.

That was all in January.

The next fall I called June and asked her if she would be interested in doing a play on the Florida circuit, in Palm Beach and Miami. She said she would if we could find the right play, but definitely not *Janus*. I sent her a number of scripts, among them *Sabrina Fair*, but she didn't like any of them. Finally on an off-chance I sent her a play I had just written called *Goodbye Ghost* in which she would play a dual role, that of a drab middle-aged suburban housewife and that of a glamorous ghost who haunts the wife's Westchester home. She fell instantly in love with it, but again, on the phone, there was the insecurity.

"Don't you think I can play it?" she asked.

"Of course I think you can play it."

"Then why didn't you send it to me before?"

I made arrangements to open the play under what seemed ideal circumstances, a special Christmas and New Year's engagement at the Little Theatre on the Square in Sullivan, Illinois, a tiny town totally removed from big city critics and big city pressures. It had been a successful summer theater operation, but had never tried a winter booking of any kind and Guy Little, the enterprising and delightful producer was very eager to make the experiment, especially with June Allyson. It was a complete success in every way. The notices were unanimously excellent and business was a complete sellout for the two and a half weeks. In spite of this, June turned to me when the curtain fell on opening night and said word for word exactly what she had said at Paper Mill.

"I am convinced I am a complete and absolute failure in this play. Maybe I'm just a complete and absolute failure, period."

As each new favorable notice came out I took it to her but she remained unconvinced and unreassured.

An opening night is an enormous pressure in the theater and I don't think the general public has ever really understood just what these pressures really are. Obviously it isn't stage fright. Most of us don't have stage fright at this late date in our careers. It is career fright. It is sheer economic fright. Especially in the case of a Broadway opening we are laying everything on the line on the basis of one single performance. If it works that night we will be active and successful for the next several years. If it doesn't work we are right back on unemployment the following day.

Those of you not in the theater, I am sure, often have the equivalent of an opening night in your private lives. You have been working on a project for two years. Finally the day comes when you submit it to your employer or your board of directors. On that one day, possibly in one hour, two years' work is accepted or rejected. Sometimes so firmly rejected that you may wonder not only whether you still have the project, but whether you still have your job. Or you may finally turn in your master's thesis to your professor and he may say, probably in other words, that it stinks.

This is a humiliation. But it is a private humiliation. When an actor fails on an opening night it is a public humiliation. He has to read about it in every newspaper the next day. Hear about it on every television channel that night. And often, six weeks later, he is still reading about it when the monthly magazines come out and the show has already long since gone.

Opening night nerves present themselves in different ways to different people. I have worked with actors who shook physically for the first five minutes after they walked onstage. I have heard very virile men open their mouths on an opening night and have their voices go up three octaves so that you would think they were playing *Charley's Aunt*. And I myself saw Ralph Forbes, on the opening night of *A Goose for the Gander* in Chicago, throw up three times in the wings and then walk onstage and be quite debonair and charming.

Obviously opening nights presented a special trauma for a

sensitive lady like June. All our problems on the tour of *Goodbye Ghost* seemed to occur on opening nights.

On opening night in Kennebunkport, Maine, for some reason June and Glenn found themselves unable to arrive at the theater until a quarter to ten in the evening. This was for an eight-thirty curtain and the curtain finally went up at ten minutes after ten for an audience who had been sitting restlessly in their seats for over an hour and a half. June's entrance reception was much less friendly than usual, to put it mildly, but she gave them that bewildered troubled little girl smile and she had them eating out of her hand before the first act curtain fell. And even well after midnight the reception on the final curtain calls was tremendous. One just wonders when she has this magic why she is so insecure about it.

On the opening night of the play in a large tent in Indianapolis the management of the theater came back at the second act intermission and gleefully announced that we had broken their all-time single performance attendance record. They invited June and Glenn and me out after the theater, but June and Glenn wanted to get back to their hotel.

I went with the management to the restaurant next door and was with them when an urgent phone call came for them at one-fifteen in the morning. It was from June and Glenn. They were at the airport leaving immediately for Hollywood. Why? They got back to their hotel and the beds weren't made.

Now that is obviously an idiotic reason. And, equally obviously, not the reason at all, though in the month that followed, even under the most relaxed and intimate circumstances, I was never given another one. But who knows what the pressures of that particular opening night were? Who knows whether June might have overheard from a stagehand or an apprentice the same kind of careless remark Margaret Sullavan heard in that television studio. The unmade bed wasn't the reason: it was just the fuse that exploded the opening night nerves.

We had a scheduled opening night at the Coconut Grove Playhouse in Miami and we had a week's layoff before the engagement there. June and Glenn went to the islands for the week and on Thursday night I got a happy phone call from June saying they would be flying in by private plane the next afternoon for final brush-up rehearsals and would I meet them at the airport.

I was at the airport early, early enough to hear a radio request for an ambulance and a stretcher. I didn't waste much time wondering for whom. June was taken off the plane on a stretcher and as she passed me she said, "I probably won't get there before, but I'll definitely be there opening night." And she was.

The management at Paper Mill bet me before we opened that we'd never get eight performances out of the play. They were wrong. Though it was nip and tuck and although I aged many years, June never missed a single one of the one hundred and forty performances of *Goodbye Ghost*. And I was grateful. And still am. And enormously sympathetic about many of the insecurities.

Katharine Cornell wrote me a letter after her husband, Guthrie McClintic, had died and she had retired to live in Martha's Vineyard. I had written asking her whether she would do a ten-week summer tour of her favorite play, any play of her choice, and with a cast of her choice, and she wrote back as follows:

Dear Mr. Kennedy,

I am most appreciative of your offer to do a ten week summer tour of my favorite play. I would like to say that I could do it. I would even like to say that I would like to do it. But the sad truth is that I have no desire to act again.

Unlike many actresses who are extremely nervous on opening nights I find that I was nervous almost every night that I ever walked on the stage. I am now fully enjoying my retirement and a freedom from all those nerves and pressures.

When Guthrie was alive his enthusiasm and his belief in me and his great sense of theatrical excitement and adventure gave me a confidence I no longer have without him. I would not only be unwilling but I think really unable to undertake such a project.

It is always nice to be thought of and so fondly remembered. I am grateful but regretful.

Sincerely,
Katharine Cornell

When June married Dick Powell he was already a major star and he went on to become one of the most successful producers and directors in Hollywood. I am told that he personally supervised all of June's activities and it may well be that it is his guidance and encouragement she misses so much and that contribute to the total insecurity.

Insecurity is always sad but it is especially so when it is unwarranted. The audiences adore June today as much as they ever did. She is something very special for them and always will be, a bright reminder of a happier and more innocent time. I wish she could relax and enjoy the affection of her audiences. But she can't. And whatever problems she gave me I know she unwittingly gave even more to herself. As a fellow actor I understood and was and still am simpatico. I guess I'm part of her audience too.

ROBERT RYAN

The following is the eulogy which I wrote for Robert Ryan at the request of the New York *Times* and which was published in the Sunday drama section of the *Times* July 15, 1973, the week after his death.

ROBERT RYAN 1909–73

BY HAROLD J. KENNEDY

Robert Ryan was a beautiful actor and an even more beautiful human being. Though his fame was as a film actor, his real love was the legitimate stage and he would do a good part in a good play any time, anywhere, and for nothing—which he usually did.

Before Off Broadway was acceptable, he did "Coriolanus" for John Houseman at the old Phoenix Theater. That was 1954. In 1958, he did "Tiger at the Gates" in Los Angeles for me at the stock minimum salary of $40 a week. He played both "Othello" and "Long Day's Journey Into Night" at the Nottingham Repertory Theater in England for $180 a week. He last worked on the New York stage in 1971 in the Off Broadway revival of "Long Day's Journey."

And it was Bob's own idea that he should do "The Front Page" on Broadway in 1969 for the Equity minimum of $167.50 per week. This then opened the door to the kind of all-star cast no normal commercial production could afford.

He was the spark plug of "The Front Page." He never came to the theater without the urgent desire that that night's performance be the best. "The Front Page" was a joyous experience for all of us. I recall only one disagreement during the entire run: a violent argument between Robert Ryan and Helen Hayes over the star dressing room. Not the kind of argument you would expect but typical of the two people involved. Neither one of them would touch it.

Miss Hayes maintained that Mr. Ryan was the star of the play and she was not about to usurp his dressing room. Mr. Ryan contended he wasn't going to loll around in a ground-floor dressing room while the first lady of the theater climbed the stairs. A hastily made, rather flimsy set of drapes solved it. We hung them across the middle of the room and Mr. Ryan and Miss Hayes shared the star dressing room with the same grace that they shared the stage.

As Walter Burns in "The Front Page," Mr. Ryan delivered one of the most famous curtain lines in the American theater: "The son of a bitch stole my watch."

When he finally left the play, the company gave him a party in the basement of the Ethel Barrymore Theater. There in the room where we had shared his 59th birthday and Thanksgiving and Christmas, we hung a huge banner, paid for and signed by the entire company. It said simply:

"Robert Ryan—The son of a bitch stole our hearts."

Bob Ryan was a senior at Dartmouth when I was a freshman there, but we never met at college. I think, however, that Dartmouth always provided an initial bond between us. Essentially private people we have always had a special awareness of the Shangri-La that is Hanover, New Hampshire. Bob Ryan was the most private person I have ever known.

In the later years, especially after 1969 when we did *The Front Page* together on Broadway, I knew him probably as well as anybody ever had except, of course, his immediate family, for whom he saved privately, exclusively, and even almost jealously a huge private chunk of himself.

His theatrical life was never allowed to interfere with his family life. Although I had two drinks with him every single night after the performance of *The Front Page* and although I went many times to his house on matters connected with the production, I was never asked to a family dinner or lunch and quite frankly I never expected to be.

The two drinks that we had after the show every night at his insistence seemed to serve as a bridge for him from the theater back to private life. After the excitement of the play he wasn't quite ready to go home. Yet he refused to go to Sardi's or any other theatrical hangout. We went every night across the street to the Gaiety Delicatessen where he had two beers, never any more, and I had two scotches. Then he would go home and I would be off to Sardi's and Joe Allen's and my other theatrical haunts.

"I'm sure it's a bore for you," Bob used to tell me, "and you'd rather be at Sardi's or some glamorous spot." But it wasn't a bore. I enjoyed the quiet, intimate relaxation of those two shared drinks every night enormously. Interestingly enough, in the course of a year no one else was ever asked to join us.

As a matter of fact, though he was extremely relaxed and friendly with the whole company backstage, I don't think Bob ever had lunch or dinner or a drink with anyone else in the company during the entire run. He gave one large cocktail party for the entire company shortly after the opening, and that was it, period. Except for his family he was a complete loner.

I first met Bob in 1951 when I asked him to meet me at Lucey's Restaurant opposite the old RKO Studio in Hollywood to discuss doing a play for me. When he walked through the door I was amazed at how tall he was, a strikingly handsome figure. Every head in the place turned. The ladies were noticeably titillated.

Bob always had an enormous appeal for the ladies for obvious reasons and for two very special ones. In the first place, he represented one of the last in a line of unassailably virile leading men. And secondly, he was almost totally unavailable.

This unavailability whetted the appetite of more than one lady star. Bob told me about an experience on an Atlantic crossing when a very big and very glamorous lady star finally collared him on deck. She had been making subtle passes at Bob the whole passage, although she was traveling with her husband. Now, on the last night out, she finally caught up with him when he was alone on deck.

After a couple of tentative forays she apparently decided that this was her last chance so she leaped at him, knocked him down, then either fell or jumped on top of him, a position she apparently did not find unattractive, as she made no effort to get up. While Bob was trying gently to disengage himself without hurting her, her husband, a crackerjack cameraman, materialized on the deck, lifted her up, reached down and took hold of Bob's shoulder, assisted him to his feet, brushed off his jacket, and then, after apologizing to him profusely, blackened both of the lady's eyes. She was between pictures, fortunately, because she stayed that way for several weeks.

I'm sure Bob must have slipped once or twice over the years, but basically he just wasn't interested. The only hint of wild oats I ever saw was one night at a cast party celebrating the success of *Tiger at the Gates*. It was strictly cast, with no outsiders. The liquor flowed more than freely and the actors were as totally relaxed as they only are when they are left entirely to themselves.

There was an actress in the company who had a very substantial crush on Bob. They had enjoyed working together, and as the party went on and the liquor spouted they eventually disappeared and were notably absent when goodbyes were said.

I staggered home and was awakened at nine o'clock in the morning by Bob, who strode into my living room, sat on the couch, took a firm hold of it, and said, "I've been on this couch all night."

"Fine," I said.

"I wish I had been," he said. "I'm a square and I should stick to typecasting."

He then lay down on the couch. "Anyway, this is where I've been," he said. "In case you're asked."

"I don't think I'll be asked," I said. And I never was.

Anyway, I was enormously impressed with him when he walked into Lucey's. I remember Helen Hayes saying to me years later when Bob played Antony to Katharine Hepburn's Cleopatra at Stratford, "What a joy it is to see a real man playing Antony." And that's what he was, a real man.

We exchanged pleasantries and talked about Dartmouth a bit. Then I got down to business and asked him if he would star for me in my West Coast production of *Detective Story*. That was when I got the first example of the complete honesty which I later grew to admire so much.

"It wouldn't interest me at all," Bob said. "Quite frankly, that's the kind of thing I get paid $200,000 a picture for doing. If I'm going to work in the theater, and for no money, I have to have a chance to do something I would never be allowed to do in films, and that probably would never be done in films. If you ever have such a property, send it to me and I'll do it for nothing."

I was committed to *Detective Story* and went ahead and did it with Chester Morris and Lydia Clarke. It was an enormous success. Bob came to see it and said he was very impressed with my directing. He added that he would like to work with me sometime if we ever could find an interesting enough property.

I went back East, and when I returned to Hollywood in 1957 I had just such a property. I had decided to do the West Coast premiere of *Tiger at the Gates*, a highly poetic, lyrical play by Giraudoux, translated by Christopher Fry. I thought it ought to be right down Bob's alley. I called him at his ranch one day and asked if I could send over the script. The ranch was in North Hollywood and it seemed as though the messenger who had delivered the script had just barely walked back into my office when the phone rang and it was Bob saying:

"Now you're talking my language. I would pay you for the privilege of saying beautiful words like these. When do we start rehearsals?"

With Bob as top star we lined up a marvelous cast, all working for the Equity Little Theatre minimum of forty dollars a week. John Ireland, Mary Astor, Marilyn Erskine, and Ray Danton were co-starred and some of Hollywood's best character actors were enlisted to support them.

We decided to break it in for a week at the Sombrero Theatre in Phoenix, Arizona, and that almost proved our undoing. I don't know what the audiences in Phoenix expected. With Bob Ryan and John Ireland, probably something like *Detective Story*. But they sure as hell weren't ready for Christopher Fry and blank verse and *Tiger at the Gates*. They stormed out in droves during the first act and fled to the bar, which set a new liquor record for the night. Those few who bothered to come back for the second act brought double scotches and double bourbons with them.

We had what was supposed to be a celebration supper in the restaurant adjoining the theater after the show. It would have made a wake seem like a hilarious clambake. The manager of the theater, not noted for his charm, told Bob and me that it was the worst show they had ever had there and would probably result in the closing of the theater. We all went to bed discouraged.

Bob was in my hotel room at nine-thirty the next morning, plunged in perspiration. "Why are you perspiring so?" I asked. After all, it was Phoenix in January.

"Flop sweat," he said, and he meant it.

"I don't think we're a flop," I said. "We planned this play for Hollywood and I think the Hollywood audience will like it.

Here in Phoenix you have the regular weekly subscribers and they come to everything, including *Getting Gertie's Garter*. This is definitely not their cup of tea. In Hollywood they'll know what they're coming to see."

There was a thud in front of my door. The morning paper. The thud seemed prophetic. I opened it. A smashing, electric, absolutely rave review. The sweat on Bob's brow cleared up a little. When the afternoon paper arrived and was even better, it was June in January in Phoenix again.

I was right about the Hollywood audience. We opened there the following Sunday night at a preview for Bob's special school in the valley which he and Jessica had founded. The audience knew exactly what to expect. They were prepared for the poetry and the imagery. And on Monday night it opened for the general public to rave reviews and a complete, absolute sellout for the entire engagement, with even Bob and myself unable to purchase one single additional seat.

That, of course, is the only kind of success that Hollywood understands. If they can get in to see something out there they figure it isn't worth getting in to. The moment they can't get in, they have to.

I had to turn down Howard Hughes, who wanted four seats for a Saturday night: we simply didn't have them. He sent a huge black limousine to the theater an hour and a half before the performance and as people arrived with their paid-for tickets his chauffeur offered them $50.00 apiece for their tickets. Since in those days the top price was $2.75 a seat that was a very substantial profit. So Mr. Hughes eventually wound up with his four seats and four ticket holders missed out on an evening of culture but pocketed $200.00.

We could have run *Tiger at the Gates* indefinitely, but Bob was committed to a movie, which we had known from the beginning. He was the only actor who was irreplaceable, so we closed on schedule, turning away several hundred people a night.

After that I didn't see Bob for a long time until he came to

New York to star in *Mr. President,* not a happy experience for him. He had very few Hollywood traits, but one of them was the horror of failure. That same "flop sweat" from *Tiger at the Gates. Mr. President* was not a success but because of all the big names connected with it the advance sale was enormous and it struggled on on Broadway for about six months. Bob hated playing it because he felt it was a failure, and that the people who came to see it felt cheated.

In New York we are inured to failure. There's almost no one of any stature who hasn't been in a couple of flops. That's the way it is. And we accept it philosophically. But Hollywood can't stand failure and if you have a failure there it is sometimes difficult to get a seat in a restaurant or even on a bus.

The only other Hollywood trait I ever observed in Bob was his firm insistence that he never read the notices of anything in which he appeared. "Kate Hepburn taught me that," he used to boast proudly. "I never read one of them."

That is a favorite Hollywood pose and Katharine Hepburn is indeed the only star of whom I think it might conceivably be true. I never called Bob on it, but in the year's run of *The Front Page* at one time or another he quoted to me every notice that had ever been written about the play, including some even I had never seen; they were so obscure they must have been printed on a hand press out on Staten Island.

Bob went back to Hollywood right after the closing of *Mr. President.* His movie career had not been going well and he changed agents. I remember his telling me about the change; it was a typical Hollywood story and, quite perversely, it worked.

"I think I'm asking too much money," he had told his new agents.

"No. You're not asking enough," they told him. So they upped his salary and he got a great deal more work. Hollywood logic—which is of course not the same as the basic logic we had both learned at Dartmouth.

It was in the summer of 1968 that I next had occasion to make serious contact with Bob. I was playing in East Hampton, Long Island, with Morey Amsterdam in a revival of *Room Service* when I read in the newspapers about a new acting group called the Plumstead Playhouse, founded by Martha Scott and utilizing the services of a number of stars, including Bob, Henry Fonda, Estelle Parsons, John McGiver, Anne Jackson, Jo Van Fleet, and others who were planning to do two shows in repertory in Mineola, Long Island. Henry Fonda was to be the principal star in the revival of *Our Town* and Bob was to be the major star of *The Front Page*.

The Front Page was a play I had been in love with for many years, having played in it with great success many times. I first played the part of Bensinger, the hilarious hypochondriac reporter, at Princeton in the summer of 1947 with Dane Clark as Hildy Johnson. I then did it again with Dane at East Hartford, Connecticut, in 1949 and in 1951 I had the great joy of directing and playing it with Pat O'Brien, who had been the Walter Burns in the first road company of the original Broadway production and had also been the Hildy Johnson in the first talking film version. Fascinatingly enough, in the film version Pat had been given the role of Hildy by mistake, as the film's producer thought that was the role he had played on the stage. Anyway, Pat knew the original play backward and forward. We also had in our company Allen Jenkins, who had been in the original Broadway production. My association with these two taught me a great deal about the play itself. We eventually did a revival of it in Hollywood with both Pat and Allen Jenkins in 1959 and though the notices were on the whole pretty good, it was not a success.

As soon as I read that Bob was doing the play I wrote him in New York at the Dakota and sent him my notices as Bensinger and said how much I would like to do the part with him. He called me almost immediately and said he would love to have me and that the only possible hitch would be if Henry Fonda, who had the choice of any supporting role, should decide he wanted to play Bensinger, which seemed to both of us unlikely.

Robert Ryan

I said that Mr. Fonda should play McCue, which is what he subsequently chose. A few days later Bob phoned me and said he had talked to Martha Scott and that I was definitely set for Bensinger.

He called me a couple of days later and said he had a funny story to tell me. Apparently he had had a phone call from Martha Scott the preceding day and it had gone like this:

"Bob," said Martha, "Leo doesn't think Harold Kennedy is right for Bensinger."

"Who is Leo?" asked Bob.

"Leo is the director of the play."

"Oh," said Bob. "Well, maybe Leo wouldn't think I was right either. Why don't we just forget about it." And he hung up.

The phone rang again in less than two minutes. Martha had just talked to Leo and apparently Leo had been confused. He must have been thinking of some other Harold J. Kennedy. Now that he thought it over he figured this Harold J. Kennedy would be perfect for it.

It turns out that Leo was Leo Brady, a director of dramatics at Catholic University, and when I arrived at the first rehearsal I discovered that the supporting cast was largely composed of recent graduates from his classes. Leaving aside their talent, which is always a matter of opinion, it was a painfully obvious and undeniable fact that most of them were too young to play the hard-bitten, jaded, beaten, bitter bastards that Hecht and MacArthur had so lovingly created for this play. And of course when they came up against Bob Ryan and Henry Fonda they looked like the Rover Boys scurrying around to get out the junior prom issue of their high school weekly.

Nor did I find them especially dedicated to their work. I was the only actor who came to the first rehearsal knowing my lines. Granted that I had played the play before, it had been nine years since the last time and the lines were hardly tripping on the tip of my tongue. I had done my homework. No one

[133]

else had. I am not being sarcastic when I say that I seriously think several of them had not even read the play before that first rehearsal.

Nor did circumstances change a great deal in the next few days. We would have a three-week rehearsal period, half of it without Bob and Henry Fonda, who were at the same time rehearsing *Our Town*. *Our Town* was to open first and when that was safely open and had played a couple of performances Bob and Henry Fonda were slated to begin attending our rehearsals. Since they were working in two plays at the same time and would still be performing *Our Town* at night and for two matinees, I assumed that the point of our early rehearsals was to get everything else out of the way and be able to concentrate on them when they joined us.

Rehearsals were leisurely, to put it mildly. I have never worked in college or regional theater and I am told that this is the pattern there. I have always worked under conditions where time was money and couldn't be wasted. As I mentioned earlier, when I did *The Front Page* on Broadway I was, because of the budget, allowed a total of only ten days' rehearsal. Every actor came to the first rehearsal knowing every line and by the fourth day we were in full performance run-throughs. The fourth day of rehearsal of the Mineola production was like a first reading by the Drama Guild of the Ladies' Sewing Circle.

In the first act of the play there is one of the most difficult card games ever played onstage. It is perfectly written, down to the last syllable, and if you play it syllable by syllable and beat by beat it will come out correctly.

Eleven hands of poker are played during the first part of the act. During these eleven hands the players shuffle, deal, place bets, draw cards, put down chips, pick up chips; someone wins, someone loses, and there is then a new deal. And all this time the players are also answering their phones and dictating routine news stories. On the first two days of rehearsal for the Broadway production I spent almost eight hours on staging this particular scene, orchestrating it almost like a symphony. And during the whole rehearsal period whenever there was a lull or a break the poker players were sent off to the basement of the Barrymore Theatre to rerun that poker game.

The fourth day of rehearsal of the Mineola production I was shocked to see the poker players still holding their scripts, not using cards or chips, and in no way working on the intricacies of this scene. Fortunately my character, Bensinger, wasn't involved in the poker game and I just went my own way and stayed out of it. When I am not the director of the play and merely an actor in it, you can't persuade me to give the director an opinion on the weather. I said nothing, but I couldn't help wondering what Bob Ryan and Henry Fonda were going to say.

I found out fast enough at the first rehearsal on the stage of the theater at Mineola to which we commuted for the final ten days of rehearsal.

Bob was not in the first act, except as an offstage telephone voice. At least he wasn't supposed to be in it. He was certainly in it at that first run-through in Mineola. I play most of the act seated in front of a large roll-top deck in the corner and we hadn't been twelve minutes into the act when I was startled to see Bob Ryan's angry face appear directly above my roll-top desk.

"What have these people been doing for ten days?" he hissed. Then he disappeared.

The face again. "Is that little boy playing one of the reporters?" he asked. "He ought to be playing the newsboy in *Our Town*."

A few minutes and then the face again. "Are we doing *John Brown's Body*? Is this a staged reading? Doesn't anybody ever put his script down?"

I didn't know Henry Fonda and had had only a cursory introduction to him from the stage manager before the rehearsal began. I had no idea what his reaction might be. He was very much a part of the act and he went through his part with what I would call an air of glazed disbelief.

He came up to me after they called "curtain."

"Have you done this play before?" he asked.

"Yes I have, Mr. Fonda."

"Well, it's obvious. You're the only one up here who knows what the fuck he's doing." And he retired to his dressing room.

By the time we got to Bob's entrance in the second act he was in a rage. His entrance comes at the peak of the dramatic action and is a fast-driving, hard-riding scene which builds to a breathless climax.

On Bob came, without a script, delivering every line with machine-gun precision. And each line was a bullet in Hildy Johnson's heart. Anthony George, who was playing Hildy, just slumped down breathless on the floor when they finally called "curtain."

"That's how we're going to do it," said Bob. "Now let's get to work." He was whistling in the dark and he knew it. That was how *he* was going to do it. And that was how Mr. Fonda was going to do it. And Estelle Parsons probably. And Anne Jackson. But that wasn't how everybody was going to do it. Because everybody quite simply wasn't up to doing it like that. As rehearsal began to improve under the determined drive of the two major stars the gulf between the principal stars and some of the members of the supporting cast became even more painfully obvious. It was almost like two separate casts in two separate plays and most of the subsequent newspaper notices made reference to that.

Bob was immensely discouraged by all this but I think what soured him completely on the Mineola production was an experience he had with one of the members of what he called the "college" cast. It was World Series time and one of the actors, playing a rather important part, spent all his time in the basement of the theater at Mineola watching the ball games. As a result, he missed his entrance in rehearsals five consecutive times. I cannot imagine why Leo allowed this. I don't know why he didn't take his cue from the look on Bob's face the second time, let alone the fourth time. Leo is a sweet man. But there is a time for a director not to be sweet, and when a careless actor is jeopardizing the production that is certainly the time.

Bob paid very little attention the first time the boy missed the entrance. He was slightly annoyed the second time. He gave Leo a look of "what are you going to do about this?" the third time. He slammed the ashtray down on the desk the fourth time. And the fifth time he walked directly down to the footlights and called out to Leo in the front of the theater:

"If that boy is one second late for one more entrance I am walking out of this play."

I don't think Leo knew it and I don't think the boy knew it, but I knew that he meant it.

I would like to be able to say that this threat electrified both Leo and the boy. It didn't particularly. Leo apparently gently reprimanded him. If I had been in the boy's shoes I would have stayed glued to the side of the stage for the rest of rehearsals. Not him. He went right back to the cellar and watched the ball games. But he was wise enough to post a buddy to stand guard and give him a two-minute warning before each of his scenes. I thought two minutes was pushing his luck quite considerably.

Bob resented the boy's attitude, but he resented even more the fact that Leo took no strong position about it and that he himself had been forced to take a stand.

Bob's final feeling about it was this: "Acting is a matter of taste. I think some of the actors in this company are not very good. But that's a matter of opinion. I could forgive them for not being very good if I thought they were dedicated or devoted to what we're doing. It's bad enough to have sloppiness in the commercial theater, but when we are doing a play, as we're doing it, for the love of doing it and for no money at all, I expect a spirit and an enthusiasm that I don't find in this company or in this production. Wouldn't you think that boy who is downstairs watching the World Series would give his eye teeth to come up and watch Henry Fonda and Estelle Parsons and Anne Jackson and John McGiver work? What does he want to be, an actor or a ballplayer? He could learn more watching Hank Fonda in rehearsal for half an hour than he could learn at the Actors Studio in twenty years."

Disenchanted though he was, Bob continued to work very hard on the play and on his role as Walter Burns. But there were some performances he really did not like and some people he found it difficult to work with. There were also a couple of performances he loved. He never tired of standing in the wings, roaring with laughter at John McGiver, playing the pompous mayor, and Charlie White playing the befuddled, totally inept sheriff. These were almost the only two people we retained for the Broadway production.

The show opened on schedule and got, on the whole, pleasant notices. Although the discrepancy in the caliber of the cast was mentioned, the reviews for the play itself were affectionate and especially good for Bob, Henry Fonda, John McGiver, Charlie White, and myself. There was nothing about the notices, however, that would make anyone consider moving it three miles out of Mineola. Martha Scott had some talk of bringing it into the City Center in New York for a special two-week run, but the distance from Mineola to Broadway is a long one and Bob said absolutely no.

The two weeks passed pleasantly and uneventfully. Business was good but not as good as it should have been with such a stellar cast. On the closing night Bob and Henry Fonda gave a "wrap-up" party at a local restaurant. There were some particularly delicious clams casino and I remember Bob swallowing one, chasing it down with a slug of beer, and saying, "Well, that buried that." I thought that that was the end of *The Front Page.*

Not so. He waited five days, which he figured was a respectable mourning period, then called me up and asked me to come over to the Dakota. As always, when I got there you would have thought he lived alone. No trace of Jessica or the family. They stayed completely out of his theatrical life. Bob got right to the point.

"I want to do this play and this part in New York. I don't care whether I do it on Broadway or off. I don't care whether I get paid one penny of salary. I only care that every part is played by a first-rate, disciplined actor. I want you to direct it and play your own part. I want no one from the Mineola production except John McGiver and Charlie White. (Henry Fonda had already indicated that he would not be interested in doing his part in New York.) I want you and me to have complete artistic control. Now you go away for a couple of days and come back and tell me how to do it."

I needed the couple of days. A forty-one-year-old play with a cast of twenty-four is not the best bait in the world for your average investor. There were no movie rights. Martha Scott had already very shrewdly tied up the television rights. A cast of twenty-four in a straight play is almost prohibitive in today's theater.

First, I investigated the off-Broadway situation. Under these conditions it made no sense at all. No matter how we tried to keep costs down, we could have sold out every performance in an off-Broadway theater and still lost money.

The only way to do it on Broadway would be to do it strictly for artistic reasons. If Bob wanted a brilliant actor in every part, then there should be a star in every part. And the only way to afford that was to ignore the question of money entirely. Have every star and every actor play at Equity minimum, which was then $167.50 a week.

I knew this would be agreeable to Bob and if he was only getting $167.50 a week how could anyone else ask for more? If people were going to work for that kind of money it would obviously have to be a limited run and I decided four weeks would be perfect. So no actor was asked to commit himself for more than four weeks, which is why when we had the surprising year-long run we eventually had so many replacements and

[139]

so much reshuffling of the cast. Many people who committed themselves for four weeks had prior commitments for a later time.

The budget obviously was a big problem. I called Robert Ludlum, now the highly prolific and enormously successful writer of best-sellers but at that time the manager of the Playhouse-on-the-Mall in Paramus, New Jersey, and asked him whether, if I gave him Bob Ryan and a cast of similar star names, all at minimum, for a two-week break-in engagement prior to Broadway, he would, in return for the savings on the salaries, provide and pay for the Broadway set and pay all the rehearsal costs. He was delighted to do so. As a result of this, when I was eventually ready to offer the project to a possible New Yorker producer I was able to offer an all-star cast, all at minimum, and the full physical production and all of the re-hearsal costs fully paid for. This amounted to a saving of at least $35,000.

I took my plan to Bob and he was delighted. He said he felt morally bound to give Martha Scott first crack at producing the package but that he would have to make it clear to her that she would have nothing whatever to say about the casting or the artistic production of the play. Martha was not interested under those conditions and I started on a list of ten producers I had drawn up who, I thought, might be good possibilities.

First one on the list was Richard Barr, who had discovered Edward Albee and produced all his plays, and was enjoying a current success with a hit production of *The Boys in the Band*. I outlined the plan to Dick and he said he didn't think he'd be interested but that he thought his partner on *The Boys in the Band*, Charles Woodward, might be and he would talk to him about it. Fifteen minutes later I got a call from Charles Woodward asking me to meet him for lunch at Sardi's and by two o'clock we had made a production deal. Subsequently Dick Barr decided he was interested after all and they did it under their Theatre 1969 production company (Richard Barr,

Charles Woodward, and Edward Albee) as a nonprofit enterprise in behalf of their new playwrights company.

Thanks to our deal with Paramus and the actors' salary concessions, they opened the play on Broadway at the Ethel Barrymore Theatre for a total cost of $19,000, exclusive of bonds, an almost unheard-of figure in today's market where in this current season a simple one-set, eight- or ten-character play costs $250,000 to $300,000 to open.

Casting was the next problem. All the agents were singularly uncooperative. "I'm not going to ask my stars to work for $167.50," most of them said. And so it wound up that in a cast of twenty-four, only one actor, Bert Convy, was cast by an agent. All the rest were people I contacted personally.

The only person who ever turned us down because of the money was Van Johnson and I must say, fond of him though I am, I think he made a very serious mistake. People in America who haven't seen him do *The Music Man*, which he did with great success on the London stage, have no idea what a first-rate stage actor he is. He did a production of *Night Must Fall* for me at the Grist Mill Playhouse in 1958 and was absolutely brilliant. He would have been a great Hildy Johnson and he could certainly use a Broadway success. But "I don't act without my money" was what he said to me. "And that's it." So he goes on endlessly playing *Boeing-Boeing* and *Send Me No Flowers* in any dinner theater or chautauqua that will pay him.

No one else made a problem of any kind about money.

"What is Robert Ryan getting?" was the first question I was always asked.

"167.50," I would say.

"Well, then, it's okay with me," was always the answer. Equity has something called a "favored-nation" clause which can be put in an actor's contract and guarantees him that no one in the production is getting or can get higher terms than he is getting, and we used these in all the star contracts on *The Front Page* very successfully.

When it came to a question of billing, that was another problem. Everybody we lost, we lost because of billing. Richard Benjamin was presumably set to be our first Hildy Johnson and his wife, Paula Prentiss, was to play the ingénue lead. Dick was perfectly willing to take second-star billing to Robert Ryan but he was not willing to allow any other names to be starred above the title, including his wife, who apparently preferred to be featured under the title. This would have meant demoting Peggy Cass, John McGiver, and all the other legitimate stars to featured billing status, and of course we refused. So we got a terse wire from Dick, who was on location with the film *Catch-22*, saying simply, "Apparently *The Front Page* is not for us."

We had a brief jubilant period when we thought we had Peter Falk, who wanted to do it. It then turned out that his agent had given us the wrong availability date. He was making the movie *Husbands* with John Cassavetes and the agent gave us a date when he was supposed to be finished, which coincided perfectly with the start of rehearsals. It then turned out that that date was the finish of shooting in the United States. There were an additional eight weeks of shooting in London, so Peter Falk was out.

George Segal went right down to the line as Hildy Johnson. The money was fine. He loved the idea of the whole cast. I agreed to work with him privately for two weeks before the official start of rehearsals. But he refused to take second billing to Bob Ryan. He insisted on being billed ahead of him, so we said a reluctant goodbye to Mr. Segal.

Jason Robards was the only one of the contenders that Bob would even consider sharing first billing with and we were trying to work out some enormously complicated deal à la Beatrice Lillie and Bert Lahr in *At Home Abroad* and Irene Dunne and William Powell in the film of *Life With Father* whereby Bob's name would be first facing Times Square and Jason's would be first facing Eighth Avenue and they would alternate first and second place in the newspaper ads and in the weekly programs. In the middle of all this Jason got a picture, which may have been just as well, as I think we would all have gone crazy with the split billing.

Bert Convy was about our eighteenth choice for Hildy Johnson, but it turned out, as it often does, that he was undoubtedly the best. Although he had done *Fiddler on the Roof* and *Cabaret*, and *The Impossible Years* on Broadway I had never really heard of him. When his agent kept pushing him I did recall that I had recently read a notice of an off-Broadway play which lasted only one night but the notice of which was headed, "Bert Convy brilliant."

Bert came to see me one day, since time was running short and we had no one else in mind, and I mentioned my vague recollection of this notice.

"Let me go home and get it," said Bert. "I'd like you to read it."

So he trudged all the way home and back and brought the notice. And he was smart to do so. Because, in fact, it was indeed a glowing personal notice. And partly because of the notice, and partly because of his avid enthusiasm and partly because he was interested enough and ballsy enough to go all the way home and back, I gave him the part. I never regretted it. He wasn't at that time much of a "name" for us, though he would be today, but his performance was big star in every way.

Peggy Cass kind of fluked into the play. A happy fluke. I called her one day to ask her how to get in touch with her great friend, Jan Sterling, who was my first choice for the part of the whore, Molly Molloy. It turned out that Jan was in England.

As I was talking to Peggy an idea crept into my mind. People forget that these ladies like Peggy and Arlene Francis were first-rate stage actresses long before they became television personalities. And Peggy had been Agnes Gooch in Rosalind Russell's Broadway production of *Auntie Mame*. She was nominated for an Academy Award for the same part in the film.

But a dramatic part? Well, why not?

"Why don't you do it, Peggy?" I asked.

"Well, why don't I?" she said.

The Front Page opened on Broadway Saturday night, May 10, 1969, and received unanimously rave reviews and went on to run through the following March. I will discuss the New York production and the various colorful personalities who were in and out of it in another chapter.

But now back to Bob Ryan.

Since the opening was on a Saturday we didn't see the notices until Sunday night. The first one I saw, which I picked up on my corner at eight-fifteen Sunday night, was the *Daily News*, which had a five-column banner headline reading, "After 41 years *The Front Page* is still the best show in town." I read Clive Barnes's rave in the men's room at Joe Allen's at ten-thirty; the restaurant itself was too dark.

On Monday morning at nine-thirty my phone rang. It was Bob Ryan. He was downstairs in the lobby and wanted to come up. I wasn't dressed and I was only half-awake, but I told him to come up anyway. He came through the door with what looked like a rather substantial package wrapped in Clive Barnes's notice. I had been busy with rehearsals and the opening and I didn't even have any coffee in the house. But he sat down.

"I have something very rewarding to tell you," he said. "Naturally I didn't want you to know any of this during rehearsal, but all of my people, my agents, my business manager, my press agent, all told me I was crazy to let you direct this play. It was nothing against you personally. It was just that with a forty-one-year-old play they all felt I needed a big name director. But I was adamant. Now, of course, they're all on the phone telling me how right I was and that they agreed with me all along."

He held out the paper.

"Open it," he said.

I unwrapped the newspaper and took out one of the most delicate and exquisite figurines I had ever seen.

Robert Ryan in the 1969 Broadway revival of The Front Page. *(Photo courtesy The Bettmann Archive, Inc.)*

Harold J. Kennedy in his Broadway role as Bensinger in The Front Page.

Helen Hayes taking a curtain call with other cast members after joining the Broadway revival of The Front Page; *from left to right, Dody Goodman, Bert Convy, Helen Hayes, Robert Ryan, Peggy Cass, and Conrad Janis. (Photo by Arnold Weissberger)*

Harold J. Kennedy and Bert Convy in The Front Page. *(Photo courtesy The Bettmann Archive, Inc.)*

Bert Convy, Katharine Houghton, and Robert Ryan in The Front Page. *(Photo courtesy The Bettmann Archive, Inc.)*

Bert Convy, Doro Merande, and Conrad Janis in The Front Page. *(Photo courtesy The Bettmann Archive, Inc.)*

A scene from The Front Page. *(Photo by Arnold Weissberger)*

Art Fleming, Sylvia Sidney, Harold J. Kennedy, Maureen O'Sullivan, Katharine Houghton, and Russell Nype in the 1975 road tour of Sabrina Fair.

"Max Reinhardt gave it to me on my wedding day," Bob said. "And now I want you to have it."

Although it meant turning down several TV and film offers, Bob stayed with the play through the first week in January. In mid-December he said to me over our two drinks one night, "Well, I've had my joy with art; now I have to go out and make some money."

So he gave notice as of the end of the first week in January. I insisted on personally giving and paying for his farewell party, which was a happy-sad affair. We all knew it wouldn't be the same from then on and it wasn't. When something has been that joyous and that rewarding and that close to perfection it is hard to settle for less.

Business began to fall off. It might well have even if Bob were still in it. After all, the old war horse had made quite a run out of it. But I was not too unhappy when we finally closed after the first week in March. I was looking forward enormously to doing the play in Hollywood, as I was sure it would duplicate its Broadway success out there. Bob had agreed to do it there in the fall and all our plans were made accordingly.

We were supposed to open in mid-September, and I had already purchased my plane tickets. I was playing *Light Up the Sky* with Kitty Carlisle and Sam Levene in Ivoryton, Connecticut, in late July when I received a long distance call at the swimming pool one day. It was from Bob. He sounded very strange and very subdued. He said he would not be able to do the Hollywood production, that he was physically unable to, and that he knew how disappointed I would be, but that it was impossible.

He never used the word cancer. In fact, for the rest of his life he never mentioned the word to me. Nor did we discuss it. It was implicitly clear that he did not wish to discuss it. I knew and he knew that I knew. And he preferred to talk about other things.

When he was getting the cobalt treatments he wasn't up to

[145]

seeing people. I stopped calling him after a while because I realized he would call me when he wanted to see me and he did.

Even with the illness he worked a great deal. One night he said to me, "I want to make as much money as I can in the next couple of years. For Jessica and the family."

He did several pictures he didn't especially want to do just for the money, but he loved doing *The Iceman Cometh* and was proud of his work in it. He asked me to come over to the Dakota one night and he spent hours showing me blown-up action portraits from the film and wonderful photographic studies of all the actors in it. I had never seen him with such memorabilia from a film before. It was almost as though it were his first movie and he was in love with and in awe of everyone in it. He loved doing it; he was wonderful in it; and it was a suitable last film for him to be remembered by.

As for Jessica and the money, how often these things are taken out of our hands. I met Bob at our corner newsstand one Saturday afternoon and he was buying almost every magazine in the rack. "They're for Jessica," he said. "She isn't feeling well and we don't know what's the matter with her. But it's nothing serious."

One week later she was dead. They had taken her to the hospital, but she had been sent back home to die. Incurable cancer.

Bob was devastated by her death and for a long time neither I nor anyone else saw him at all. He did go to stay with some old friends in the country for a long time and after he came back he pretty much avoided everybody.

About a year later I began to read in the columns that he and Maureen O'Sullivan were being seen everywhere together. There were hints that it might be a romance and I certainly hoped so. And as it turned out, it was.

This lovely lady gave him all her warmth and affection and provided him with enormous comfort and happiness the last year of his life. She gave up several acting jobs to take care of him and be with him wherever he went.

When we were playing *Sabrina Fair* in Detroit two years ago,

Maureen was asked by an interviewer, "Who was the love of your life?"

"John Farrow," she said without hesitation. John Farrow was her husband and the father of her seven children, including Mia Farrow.

Then she added, "And one other."

I don't know why she was so reticent. The one other was obviously Robert Ryan. She adored him and he adored her.

The last time I saw Bob was when he and Maureen were together in his apartment at 88 Central Park West. Maureen called me about five-thirty in the afternoon and said Bob had a great yearning to see me and she was cooking dinner and could I come by and have dinner with them.

I went and Bob seemed in good health and good spirits. He had been asked to do *Shenandoah* on Broadway. He was very excited about it. Maureen cooked and served dinner and then we all sat and chatted for a couple of hours and finally Bob said he was tired and took off for bed. He seemed fine and enormously happy with Maureen and I knew he was in good hands.

That was the last time I ever saw him. Two days later he was taken to the hospital. Again incurable. Again just waiting for him to die.

Maureen was with him every minute she was allowed to be and she was with him under harrowing circumstances when he died, apparently choking to death in one of those machines that seemed to be backing up on him while Maureen ran screaming up and down the corridors for help that never came.

I had my first day of rehearsal of a new comedy called *Don't Frighten the Horses*, which I had written especially for Kitty Carlisle and in which she was starring for a summer stock tour. We had a wonderful first rehearsal and in a spirit of jubilation I stopped in at Charlie's on Forty-fifth Street, near our rehearsal hall, and ordered a Beefeater martini on the rocks.

While he was making it, the bartender, whom I had never seen before, said, "Too bad about that actor."

"What actor?" I said.

"That Robert Ryan," he said.

"What about Robert Ryan?"

"He died this afternoon."

The tears spurted straight out of my eyes. Not down my cheeks but straight, forward, and onto the bar.

The poor bartender was horrified and a little frightened about what he might have done. It is interesting how in a terrible crisis some minor detail can distract your mind for a minute or two. I was momentarily so concerned with trying to reassure the bartender, who was new and who I really think thought he was going to lose his job, that it helped me compose myself slightly.

I didn't drink the drink. I don't know whether I paid for it. I got up and walked out of the bar. And I walked up to Forty-seventh Street and stood in front of the Ethel Barrymore Theatre. I don't know how long I stayed there. I don't know whether I saw anyone or whether anyone saw me.

Then I walked to the Actors' Chapel at St. Malachy's and lit a candle.

And then I went home and stayed up all night writing the Memorial which began this chapter. Not that it is so well written that it should have taken all night to write, but simply because the New York *Times* severely restricts the number of words that can be used in a piece of this kind.

It is difficult to write about a great man in 650 words. I tried.

THE GREAT KLEENEX CAPER

Michael Todd, Joan Blondell, who was then Mrs. Todd, and I were involved in a widely publicized backstage battle at the McCarter Theatre in Princeton, New Jersey, in August 1949. It was what the trade calls a "hot weather" story. There was no noteworthy national or international news at the time so the tabloids seized upon this incident and blew it up out of all proportion. It was on the front page of both the New York *Daily News* and the *Mirror* for several days. And there were as many versions of what happened as there were papers.

Actually nobody ever got the story straight, which was not surprising. Through a series of misadventures, what actually happened made no sense at all.

The original story was that Mike Todd had beaten me up for reprimanding Miss Blondell. Then there was a story that Miss Blondell had hit me, and a counter story that I had hit her. In trying to slough it all off, Miss Blondell told the New York *Times* that she had merely thrown a piece of Kleenex at me and that was how the tabloids dubbed the story "The Battle of the Kleenex." What actually happened was that through a weird chain of circumstances Mike Todd hit Miss Blondell.

Things started off badly when the Todds arrived seven and a half hours late for the dress rehearsal of the play *Happy Birthday* in which Miss Blondell was to play the starring role originated by Helen Hayes on Broadway. The part was that of a shy, withdrawn, reticent spinster librarian.

Mike and Joan had not sent word that they were going to be late, and they never did send word, so the whole cast and crew were hanging around the theater from two o'clock Sunday afternoon until the Todds finally arrived at nine-thirty that night. Mike immediately assumed the role of big spender and sent out for a case of beer and sandwiches for the company, but that wasn't what the company wanted. They wanted and needed the rehearsal.

It was a partial package, with Miss Blondell bringing four or five actors who had done the play with her the preceding week at Ivoryton, Connecticut, and our resident company playing all the other parts. It was a large cast and a play full of trick effects. We needed every minute of the brief rehearsal time allotted, which was all day Sunday and again Monday afternoon, with the opening performance on Monday night.

With the delays and the irritation and the case of beer, Sunday night's rehearsal was pretty much a waste of time, but we did have a very good rehearsal on Monday afternoon. Our actors had done their work thoroughly and worked very well with the Blondell contingent, most of whom were quite good, and it looked as though there was every chance of a good performance on the opening night.

That night Mike Todd and I stood together at the back of the theater as the curtain went up. A few minutes into the play Miss Blondell, in the character of Addie, made her first entrance. "Addie's never had a drink in her life before," said another character, by way of introducing her.

The audience exploded with laughter. It was one of the biggest laughs I've ever heard in any theater, anywhere, anytime.

Mike grabbed my arm.

"Too titty?" he asked. "Is she too titty? Is that the trouble?"

Too titty she was, but that wasn't the trouble. Actually it wasn't Miss Blondell's fault, but it wasn't the audience's fault either. Acting in summer stock is basically making a personal appearance. An audience comes to see you do what you are known for doing. They don't expect or want any surprises.

The audience that came to see Miss Blondell had seen her and loved her as the wisecracking kind of blowzy broad in all those Jimmy Cagney and "Gold Diggers" Warner Brothers movies and it never occurred to them to take that line seriously. Helen Hayes they would have accepted it about. Not because Helen is a better actress but because that is the kind of role they would expect Helen to be playing.

As a matter of fact, Miss Blondell was very good in the play and if the line had come much later, say in the second act, after she had had a chance to establish a character, the audience wouldn't have laughed. But I'm afraid it's true that when you get a public image that is strong enough to sell tickets you are apt also to be stuck with that image. It is as though Patsy Kelly were to walk out on her first entrance and announce, "I'm Cleopatra."

Zasu Pitts always wanted to play *The Glass Menagerie* for me and would have done it without salary. I think she might well have been marvelous in it, as she gave an extraordinary dramatic performance in the silent film classic *Greed*. But I couldn't let her do it because I knew her audience would not accept it.

Zasu and Edward Everett Horton were two of the biggest box office draws in summer stock in the forties and early fifties, not only because people wanted to see them in person, which they did, but because their names guaranteed one thing to an audience. Comedy with a capital C. That was what the audience wanted from them and no matter how well they might act, there would be no point in their trying to do *The Wild Duck* or *John Gabriel Borkman*.

Naturally the unexpected audience response disturbed Miss Blondell and the members of her company, but they went on and gave a good performance and later in the play when the librarian loosened up and Miss Blondell had the chance to play an amusing drunk scene, which was more what the audience expected, things went very well indeed. But the evening was hardly an unqualified success and there was much muttering among the Blondell contingent about how much better the play was at Ivoryton, and, of course, since the actors always get blamed, how much better the actors were there.

Mike Todd went back to New York the next morning and I didn't go to the theater Tuesday night as I was rehearsing the following week's play, *The Barretts of Wimpole Street*, at the Nassau Tavern. After that evening's performance a group of my actors who were in the Blondell play stopped by my rehearsal and complained that Miss Blondell and her actors were muttering obscenities at them under their breath onstage during the performance and also giving them directions and generally pushing them around.

I called a meeting of the entire company on the stage the next day before the matinee and said quite firmly that this kind of behavior would stop immediately and served official notice to the Equity deputy of the complaints that had been made. I pointed out that we had an extremely efficient stage manager and that he was not a minion, but was in fact the supreme authority backstage. If anyone had any complaints or wanted anything corrected he was the man to do it for them.

When I had finished my whole diatribe I was amused to have Miss Blondell ask, "Now just who is this Mr. Minion?"

Our stage manager's name was Howard Miller, but for all the rest of his years at Princeton he was affectionately known as Howard Minion.

The matinee went off without incident except that the intermissions were a little long. Miss Blondell apparently spent all of them on the phone to Mike Todd in New York.

I was having dinner at the Nassau Tavern when a frightened courier from the theater came to the table and reported that Mike Todd was at the theater in Miss Blondell's dressing room and wanted to see me right away. I located the Equity deputy and together we went to the theater and backstage to Miss Blondell's dressing room.

It was a double room with an outside sitting room, and an inside makeup and dressing room. We knocked on the door. Mike Todd yanked it open. He was alone in the outside sitting room; and inside I could see Miss Blondell sitting in front of the mirror.

Mike lashed out at me in a rage, shouting, asking me who the hell I thought I was to reprimand his wife. I stood my ground very firmly and said that I personally had no quarrel with Miss Blondell, but that I was forced to act on behalf of my actors.

"You and your fucking actors," he said, and made a lunge at me. The Equity deputy, one of the mildest men I've ever known, somehow thrust himself between us and successfully averted the blow, with which Miss Blondell came raging out of the inside room and hit the Equity deputy over the head with her hand mirror.

At that Mike Todd turned on her and said, "You stupid bitch, I told you to stay out of this." Then he hauled off and belted her.

As she doubled over in pain, I fled. I am a drawing-room comedy actor and wrong for gangster movies. I'm also a complete coward and my reaction to any kind of physical violence is full flight.

So I ran out to the box office, locked myself in, and continued selling tickets until the curtain finally went up. Meantime, Mike diverted the paying customers by pounding on the box office door, threatening my life, castigating me, my actors, the town of Princeton, the University, and everything else. He was presently escorted to his room at the Nassau Tavern by the local sheriff. By the end of the evening we had all had it. Even Mike had cooled down. Although none of us ever spoke to one another for the rest of the week, I think there was a kind of tacit understanding of let's just get the week over with and get on to other things.

But the next day the newspapers started. I had never been in a situation like that before and I was fascinated and appalled by the way the tabloids worked. They would phone me and tell me terrible things Mike or Joan had said about me and ask for my comments. I'm sure they did the same thing with Joan and Mike. I clammed up but it didn't do any good.

For a couple of days there were front page stories, each more lurid than the other. The *Daily News* had a double picture over the whole front page: one half showing Joan and Mike at the Stork Club; and the other half, unfortunately, a picture of Sarah Churchill, obviously naked under a terry cloth robe, and obviously drunk, collapsed in my arms.

The caption merely said, "Joan Blondell with Mike Todd" and "Harold J. Kennedy with Sarah Churchill."

Poor Sarah. The paper didn't bother to explain that the photograph was taken from the drunk scene of *The Philadelphia Story*, which she and I had done at Princeton a few weeks before. Talk about an innocent bystander. Not only did it look as though she were obviously drunk and disorderly, but it somehow looked as though Sarah were at the bottom of the whole business instead of being happily five hundred miles away doing the same play in the relative peace and quiet of Skowhegan, Maine.

Nobody, including innocent bystanders, comes out of a shambles like this very well. If the newspapers had just left us alone, Joan and Mike and I would eventually have had a good laugh and forgotten the whole thing. But laughter and contentment don't make good tabloid copy.

The next week at Princeton I played the archvillain, Edward Moulton Barrett in *The Barretts of Wimpole Street*. The part is unsympathetic at best and I had the added disadvantage of playing it opposite the lovely Susan Peters, who had had that tragic hunting accident, and was playing the role of my daughter, Elizabeth, from her own real-life wheel chair. Nonetheless, I gave it my evil all and the audience was vastly relieved when Elizabeth and her little dog Flush escaped from my odious house.

I'm sure that Miss Blondell will be pleased to hear that a lady patron emerging from the Wednesday matinee of *The Barretts* was heard to observe:

"Well, I'm not surprised poor Joan Blondell had trouble with him."

CHARLTON HESTON

CHARLTON HESTON IS a square. But an enchanting one. It's nice in a kinky business to run up against an occasional square and a return to a few of the good old-fashioned values, maybe even the five-cent cigar. Not that Chuck is dull. He isn't. Nor lacking in a sense of humor. He is not in himself basically witty or humorous, but he is highly appreciative of humor. I can't imagine him playing Noël Coward, but he would be a great audience for it. In a largely flamboyant business, he is the least actory actor I have ever worked with. He makes Robert Ryan almost seem like Clifton Webb.

Basically Chuck is a family man. He adores his wife, the talented Lydia Clarke, who gave a lovely performance for me opposite Chester Morris in my West Coast production of *Detective Story*. And he adores his two children. But he has brought them up the way an old bachelor like myself thinks children should be brought up, to be bright and attractive human beings and not the kind of Tennessee Williams "no-necked monsters" that so many theatrical children turn out to be.

I first met Chuck when Lydia was doing the play for me and he was then at a peak of fame sizzling across the screen opposite Jennifer Jones in *Ruby Gentry*. He used to wait in the alley at the stage door of the Ivar Theatre for Lydia every night. Never came backstage. Never stuck his nose into a rehearsal. Not that he's shy. He just has good professional manners and wouldn't dream of intruding.

Like Robert Ryan, Chuck is a dedicated legitimate theater actor. I don't know how much he soaks film producers for those disaster movies he makes but I would think plenty, as they are hardly the kind of thing he would do for his soul. But when he decides to do a play in the legitimate theater, he isn't concerned about the money. All he wants is to be sure that everything is first-rate: the cast, the scenery, the costumes, the lights; that everything is as close to perfect as it can be.

He is not stupid and he doesn't want to be taken advantage of, either. Because he is doing the show primarily for love, he doesn't want to find out that he is getting less salary than someone who hasn't done a movie since *The Birth of a Nation*.

"Just get me a salary that is commensurate with what someone in my position should get and within the realm of what the management can afford," he told me.

"And get me enough money so that if there should be a first-rate actor we want and the management can't afford him, we can make up the difference out of my salary."

When he did *A Man for All Seasons* for me in Chicago I got him the top guaranteed salary that any star had ever had in summer stock and I also got him a substantial percentage over the break-even point. The percentage turned out to be a bonanza, because it was a huge theater. We sold out every seat at every performance, so Chuck walked off with a bundle.

He couldn't have cared less about that. What he did care about was that he also walked off with the Chicago Drama

Critics' Golden Straw Award as the best actor of the year; and, since he is a generous man, he was also delighted that I received the same award as best director.

It wasn't easy.

I have done plays before where the actors weren't ready, the costumes weren't there, the lights weren't there, the scenery wasn't there. I have never done a play before where the theater wasn't there.

The theater was the Mill Run Playhouse in Niles, Illinois, just outside of Chicago. It is flourishing today but it hadn't even been built when I was approached early in the spring of 1965 to provide an opening attraction for it.

Two businessmen from Chicago contacted me in New York and asked me to meet with them. They showed me plans for a gorgeous theater in the round which they said was already well under construction and for which they wanted a super opening attraction in late May. They asked me for suggestions.

I had run into Chuck and Lydia at Sardi's East in New York only a few weeks before and we had talked, as we always did, about doing a play some day. It instantly occurred to me that the site of the theater was very close to Chuck's alma mater, Northwestern University, for which he has always had a very warm regard.

"What about Charlton Heston?" I asked.

You would have thought I had suggested God, with whom, as a matter of fact, because of his countless biblical roles, Chuck is frequently confused.

Anyway, they were ecstatic over the idea. I explained to them that I knew Chuck very well and that he would only do something that he really wanted to do. They didn't care if he did *The Bat* or *Up in Mabel's Room*. I also suggested it might be a good idea if, in addition to whatever salary they offered Chuck, they threw in a scholarship in his name to some deserving student at Northwestern. They enthusiastically agreed.

I called Chuck in California and outlined the whole proposition to him. He was definitely interested. I asked him if he had any play he was especially interested in and he said he was dying to do *A Man for All Seasons*. It turned out to be the perfect choice. Contracts were signed and an opening date was set for early June. I auditioned actors in New York, lined up a really first-rate cast, and had them all fitted to some gorgeous period costumes which were shipped on to Chicago. Chuck, of course, was playing Sir Thomas More, and Lydia was playing his wife. They had their costumes done in Hollywood and brought them with them. Everything seemed more than auspicious.

About ten days before the first scheduled rehearsal, while I was still in New York, I had a call from Chuck from Hollywood.

"Harold," he said, "what do you hear about the theater?"

"What do you mean?"

"Well, I have friends who live there," he said, "and they drive by it every day and they say it is still a hole in the ground. Shall I have my agent make ugly noises?"

"Maybe you'd better," I said.

I'm sure his agent did make ugly noises and I am sure they frightened the theater management but, as we learned later, nothing frightens a building contractor.

I arrived in Niles at two o'clock in the morning the night before the first rehearsal, having driven out from New York with one of the supporting actors and my dog. With Chuck's conversation very much in mind and even before I checked in at my motel I asked a policeman if he could direct me to the theater and he gave me very specific instructions. We drove up across the street from the building and were vastly encouraged to find it a rather handsome edifice, obviously fully completed and far from a hole in the ground. I checked in at the motel and went to bed immensely relieved.

The next morning I was awakened sharply at nine o'clock by the shrieking of car brakes in the parking lot of my motel right next to my ground-floor window. I looked out. A car had come to an abrupt halt with its nose just against my windowpane, and out of the car jumped Chuck Heston. I barely got away from the window when the phone rang and it was Chuck from the lobby and would I meet him in the coffee shop. I got dressed in a hurry and there was Chuck in the coffee shop looking as though he would never get the Red Sea to part.

"Have you seen the theater?" he asked.

"Yes," I said cheerily.

"And?" he asked.

"I haven't seen the inside but the outside looked fine."

He looked at me as though I ought to be committed.

"It's a soccer field," he said.

I got vaguely uneasy.

"Where is it?" I said.

"Right across the street," he said. "You can see it from the window."

Right across the street was not where I had been last night. And when I went to bed in the motel I didn't remember anything being right across the street. I got up and looked out the window. I was right. There was nothing there. Well, almost nothing. A deep-dug soccer field. It turned out later that the night before I had seen the local movie theater.

Our theater was indeed across the street. What actually was across the street might more aptly have been called a work in progress. There were girders galore, and the skeleton of what might eventually be walls; and trucks everywhere dumping concrete, and whistles blowing and workers scurrying; but certainly nothing resembling a theater that was going to open in two and a half weeks.

I tracked down the local producers at their hotel while Chuck and I drugged ourselves with coffee waiting for them.

They came in the door talking.

"We've got a triple crew on; they're working twenty-four hours a day, and we're going to make it," they said.

"No way," I thought. And I was right.

We rehearsed very thoroughly the first few days in the high school gymnasium. Chuck was immensely stimulated by the caliber of the actors I had brought from New York and it was apparent from the outset that he himself had done his homework and was going to give a striking performance. All the other actors had also done their homework and when we had a rough complete run-through from start to finish at the end of the third day, there was no question in anyone's mind that it was going to be a first-rate production. At the end of that first run-through I gave Chuck my first piece of personal direction and I was delighted at the way he took it.

"You're awfully gloomy in that first scene," I told him.

"What do you mean, 'gloomy'?" he asked.

"Well, it's a party scene and you're the host and the wine is flowing and it ought to be very 'up,' but you're playing it as though you've already read the play and you know you're going to be beheaded in the end."

Chuck laughed. "You're absolutely right," he said. "I'm playing a definite awareness of certain things the character doesn't know yet. I'll fix it."

The next time through he gave a totally different interpretation; brighter, more alive, and in no way anticipating later events. It gave a whole new rich color and variety to his performance.

Each day at the end of rehearsal Chuck and I would drive down and gaze gloomily at the construction site. They were making progress, there was no doubt about that, and they were indeed working twenty-four-hour shifts. But each day we hoped for a miracle. One wall in place. One block of seats put in. And that didn't happen.

At the end of the first week of rehearsal Chuck asked the two producers to meet with him and me at a restaurant near the rehearsal hall. I remember there was a tornado warning and as we sat there looking out the restaurant windows there were the darkest skies and the weirdest hush I have ever witnessed. I expected the tornado to break at any moment and solve the whole problem of what to do about the theater. "Gentlemen, it's obvious we can't make the scheduled opening," Chuck said.

They nodded their heads. "We know," they said.

"What do you want me to do?"

"Give us two more weeks," the producers said. "And at the rate we're going we can definitely make it."

"I'll give you two more weeks," Chuck said, "but that's absolutely all I can manage because of other commitments. And I personally won't charge you any salary. You'll have to work out what you can with the other actors."

I felt extremely sorry for the producers, as the delay in construction obviously wasn't their fault and yet it involved enormous expense and inconvenience for them. All the rest of the actors had to be paid full salary for the additional two weeks' delay. All the rentals on lights, costumes, and so on had to be proportionally increased. All the tickets that had been sold had to be reprinted or exchanged. I don't think they could have managed it or that it would have been worth managing if Chuck hadn't contributed his end of it for nothing.

We took a couple of days off from rehearsals and Chuck went to Washington and did a poetry reading at the White House, which he had earlier been asked to do. When he came back we plunged into full rehearsals again. We had lost some ground as, due to the change in schedule, Richard Dysart had to withdraw from the role of the Common Man in which he was excellent. However, we were able to get John Heffernan, who had just won the Tony for *Tiny Alice* in New York, and a full week before the second scheduled opening of the theater the show itself was more than ready to open. It was very exciting that last week to watch the miracle begin to happen at the theater. Each morning we would leave the motel about ten-thirty to drive out to the high school gymnasium some twelve miles away, and each evening after rehearsals were over Chuck and I would drive back to the theater site. Each evening something new and exciting had been added. Half a wall had sprung up. Another huge block of seats had been installed. Finally the stage itself materialized between the time we left one morning and the time we got back that night. On the last day of rehearsal at the gymnasium, forty-eight hours before the opening performance, we got back home and found that the theater, at long last, had a roof.

The opening night was a Friday and we had given the management an ultimatum that at six o'clock on Thursday night, twenty-six hours before the curtain, every detail of construction would have to stop, whatever state it was in; all the laborers would have to go home; and the theater must finally be turned over to the actors, the director, the electricians, the costumers, the technicians, all the people responsible for the production of the play itself and no one of whom had ever yet set foot in that theater or on that stage.

As I said before, it wasn't easy.

We had our last two acting rehearsals of the play in the gymnasium on Wednesday. I wanted the actors to rest all day Thursday, as it was obvious we would be at the theater all Thursday night. I explained to them that this would be their last chance to function as actors until the actual opening night because, when we finally got into the theater, they would be reduced to virtual puppets and be totally at the mercy of the lights, the sound, the long ramps that had to be manipulated to get on and off the stage, the pit that was to be used as a dungeon, which no one had yet ever seen, and all of the physical elements of a production none of which had yet had a chance to be tested.

They understood, and in the high school gymnasium out in the middle of nowhere, twelve miles from Niles, Illinois, with no costumes, no lights, no props—with what Shakespeare called "two boards and a passion"—they gave two electrifying performances of *A Man for All Seasons* for an audience of only one, myself. It was a small but appreciative audience. I gave them what few notes I had and said that I was now through with them as actors. From now on we would all just be bodies and I urged their cooperation in getting the physical details of the production together.

At six o'clock on Thursday evening we finally got into the

theater. It was chaos, but organized chaos. No sense of panic, just a great sense of urgency.

Theater people are very aware and very sensitive. We all knew the impossible situation the producers had been placed in by the construction delay and everybody wanted to help. Actors unpacked their own costumes and lugged them up and down the ramps. People offered to stand in for the focusing of the lights. The electrician was a crackerjack. He had attended every rehearsal and worked out a meticulous light plot and in the four hours between six o'clock and ten o'clock he and his crew had hung all the lighting equipment for the play, a task that would normally have taken two working days.

Of course, the hanging of the lights was only the beginning, but a good beginning. The play was full of dimouts, fadeouts, and blackouts and these could only be worked out with the actors as the play itself progressed.

But at ten o'clock we were ready to start a formal rehearsal. We proceeded with painful slowness, going inch by secure inch. When something didn't work we went back and did it over again until it did work. The actors didn't bother with acting per se. But they used their full voices so that we could regulate the sound levels. They had to work a great deal with the ramps. When you are working in the round the entrances and exits up and down the ramps require the most meticulous planning and timing. You have to start down the aisle on an exact and specific word in order to be on stage at exactly the right second to pick up your cue. If you are a beat late the pace falters; if you are a beat early you distract from what is going on before you. Naturally we had attempted to approximate and estimate this in the gymnasium, but now we had the actual ramps for the first time. The actual lengths were different, the rake was different, and almost every entrance and exit in every scene had to be run at least five or six times.

The same was true with the lights. The dimouts and the fadeouts had to be adjusted to the rhythms of the actors' speeches, and then had to be run over again and again.

[164]

But the weeks of intensive rehearsal all paid off. Every actor knew what he was doing. When he tried it the first time and it didn't quite work he was able to figure out very easily whether to start two words earlier or three words later.

We had also rented the sound tapes of the original Broadway production and these had to be integrated into the show. Of course, no one had heard them before. It was a long and tedious night, but I never heard a voice raised nor a single snap of irritation. Coffee and sandwiches were sent in about midnight and rehearsal went on until seven-thirty in the morning. At that time I sent the actors home, remaining at the theater myself until noon rerunning the blackouts, the music and the sound and other technical things.

I went home at noon with a strange air of detachment. It is something that always happens to me when I am not also acting in a play that I have directed. If you are also appearing in the play you have the feeling, right or wrong, that there is still something you can do to help things along. When you are only directing there comes a time, before the curtain goes up, when you feel that you have done everything you can and the rest is in the lap of the gods. And I always feel not only detached but a little disloyal, as though I had deserted my actors and ought to be up there on that stage sweating it out with them. Anyway, I had a couple of hours' sleep, shaved and showered, put on a tuxedo, and went to the theater that night as a member of the audience. The theater itself wasn't really quite ready for an audience. Patrons had to walk gingerly across very precarious planks that covered all the half-set cement which had still not been cleaned up. The lobby was unfinished and full of old planks and debris of all kinds. I am told there was a slight problem with the plumbing in the ladies' room. But none of it mattered. The audience had come to see a show, and they saw one.

Everything was perfection. A director's dream. With one exception. And that exception could have destroyed the show and very nearly gave me a heart attack all during it.

As I took my seat in the auditorium I noticed a large arc light hanging over the center of the stage. It had obviously been used as a work light by the construction workers and it had obviously also been there the night before but I hadn't noticed it, as it wasn't on. Now, as the audience streamed into the theater, it was on full blast. It was perfectly all right before the show, as it helped illuminate the auditorium, but I hurried backstage to warn them to turn it off before the play began.

I found my efficient electrician in a state of panic.

"We don't know how it got on," he said. "And what's worse, we don't know how to get it off. It's obviously hitched up to the construction equipment somewhere and we can't find where."

"What about the last scene of the play?" I said.

"Oh, my God," he said. "Well, we'll find it before then."

The final scene of the play is the beheading of Sir Thomas More. It is an enormously effective scene and builds breathlessly right up to the actual beheading. At the close of the scene Chuck was to kneel down, put his head on the block; then the executioner slowly raises the axe, and as he starts to swing it downward, there is a piercing scream; and then a blackout. In the blackout Chuck ducks out from under the axe and gets off the stage in the darkness. There could not possibly be a light leak of any kind. If the audience caught a glimpse of Chuck ducking out from under the axe and sneaking off the stage, it would result in a howl of laughter that would destroy the evening. And strangely enough the more intently involved the audience was, the bigger would be the laugh. Partly release and partly a sense of the ludicrous. Too abruptly back to reality.

It was, however, the final scene of the play and still a long way away, and the electrician assured me he would not rest during the first act until he found the source of the offending light. Places had been called and the audience was already seated, so I told them to go ahead with the first act and that I would come back at intermission.

The light did no great harm in the first act, though it some-

[166]

what diminished the theatricality of the dimouts and the fade-outs. They never really worked, as there was always this one brilliant arc light burning overhead.

But audiences in the round are used to seeing actors under normal circumstances entering and exiting up the aisles and they accept such things. The act went brilliantly and there was a roar of enthusiastic applause at the end.

At intermission I went backstage. They still had not been able to locate the source of the light. They thought it might be coming from outside the building.

We're in Chicago, I thought, and surely someone in the audience has a gun on his hip. Why couldn't we just borrow it and shoot it out like they do in western movies.

Seriously, however, I had made a firm decision. After the first act had gone so brilliantly there was no way we could run the risk of a Keystone Kops finish to the evening. I told the stage manager I would go back out front for the first half of the second act and they should keep trying to kill the light. But if it was still on halfway through the act I would come backstage and cut the last scene of the play completely, ending the evening with the trial scene. I said not to tell anybody because we might not have to do it, but if all else failed that was what I was determined to do.

I went back out front and sat through the first half of the second act watching the light far more than the actors. It burned with a kind of belligerent brightness. I knew it was never going to go out. Finally I rose from my seat and started backstage to give the order to cut the final scene of the play.

Oh, ye of little faith! I had forgotten Chuck's intimate acquaintance with Moses and God. I was halfway up the ramp with my back to the stage when I heard a loud explosion. I turned around and though I will never know how or why, the arc light had exploded and burned itself out.

Chuck was in the middle of a long speech and he gave a look of mild annoyance in the direction of the sound. I thought, "Chuck, baby, that explosion is the sweetest music you will ever hear."

I went back to my seat a free man and I must say I have never enjoyed an execution more.

The play soared on through its final scene. The executioner raised the axe. He started to swing it downward. There was a piercing scream. And then total, complete, heavenly blackout. And when the lights came back up, a bare stage and a standing ovation.

I said to Chuck in his dressing room afterward:

"What did you think about that work light?"

"Well, I got kind of used to it," he said. "It didn't bother me."

"It didn't?" I said. "How were you planning to do the end of the play?"

Chuck turned paler than Sir Thomas More on the block.

"I never thought of it," he said. "I was acting the play scene by scene and I just never thought ahead. What would have happened?"

"I'll tell you exactly what would have happened," I said. "The boy playing the executioner is very eager and very 'method.' He is also your understudy. I think he would have opted for the old maxim that the show must go on. He would have figured that the play was over anyway and we really didn't need you any more. So I think he would simply have beheaded you and played the part tomorrow night."

The notices were raves; business was sellout; and Chuck and I did eventually receive the two Critics awards. But apart from the personal satisfaction, it is good for the legitimate theater itself when a major Hollywood star and a big box office attraction like Chuck is so warmly and enthusiastically received. It may eventually help to diminish the fears and misgivings about the stage many Hollywood stars have, as Cary Grant so clearly expressed. A few more awards to stars like Chuck and we might even get Cary up there. He could still call himself by an assumed name. I would suggest something nondescript like maybe Robert Redford.

THE FRONT PAGE
ON BROADWAY

When the first display ad for *The Front Page* appeared in the New York *Times* with these twelve names above the title—Robert Ryan, Peggy Cass, Bert Convy, Katharine Houghton, Conrad Janis, Val Avery, Horace McMahon, Julia Mcade, Doro Merande, Don Porter, Loring Smith, and Arnold Stang—and a total cast of twenty-four, my drinking buddies at Sardi's bar said to me, "With that group, you'll be in a sanitarium in a week."

"No, I won't," I said. "I know exactly how I'm going to do it."

The first rehearsal was called at noon at the Ethel Barrymore Theatre and exactly at twelve o'clock I had the whole company seated on folding chairs lined across the stage.

"We have twelve stars above the title of this play," I said, "and a total cast of twenty-four actors. And that's how it's going to be. Twenty-four actors, but only one director. The best way to destroy this play is to have twenty-four separate opinions about how to do it. I know how to do it. And if you find out that I don't, then get together and get me fired. But don't give me any arguments."

Nobody really ever did. Actors are like children. They like authority and respect it if someone can warrant it and maintain it. If the director cannot do this, then a series of power plays develop among the actors, always to the detriment of the play and to the destruction of any kind of unity and amity backstage.

I had one minor, very understandable clash with Peggy Cass. Peggy was playing the whore, Molly Molloy, originated in the first production by Dorothy Stickney. It is a marvelous part but a very melodramatic one. Peggy was obviously concerned about this. I felt she was holding back a little, and I told her so.

"But, Harold, it's so melodramatic," Peggy wailed.

"That's just the point," I said. "This is a comedy-melodrama. You have to play it that way. There's no sense in doing a melodrama if you're going to apologize for it. Just play the pants off it."

I don't think she was entirely convinced, but she went back up on the stage and tried her first scene again. On Molly comes and begins her tirade against the reporters. She nails them one by one. I don't know how "method" Peggy is, but I had a feeling that with each one of them she was also nailing me. It didn't matter. I never care why something works or how, just so long as it works. Peggy was absolutely electric and when she got to her screaming exit, "You lousy bastards, you dirty low-down bums," the whole company gave her an ovation.

We didn't hear any more complaints about the melodrama. "Gorgeously melodramatic" were the very first two words of Clive Barnes's review. I am firmly convinced that the success of our revival was the careful balance we kept between the comedy and the melodrama.

"The great virtues of this revival are its pace and its seriousness," said Edwin Newman in his TV review.

And Walter Kerr wrote: "Mr. Kennedy makes a fine, fussy Bensinger. And he has been right to be fussy about his actors. No one was allowed to play for a laugh. Everyone takes it deadly seriously and the results are hilarious."

This is the mistake the usually astute Billy Wilder has made in his recent film version of the play, the third and by far the least successful of its translations to the screen. Mr. Wilder was so busy having Jack Lemmon and Walter Matthau play tongue-in-cheek and camp and kid the script that when Carol Burnett as Molly Malloy jumped out the window it was the biggest laugh in the picture. Not Miss Burnett's fault. You can't kid a melodrama and then expect the audience to take it seriously at some moment of your own choice. They didn't laugh in New York when Peggy Cass jumped out that window.

The first performance in New York was an invitational preview to which all of the cast were allowed to invite their friends. I dreaded it. Friends are an actor's worst possible audience. If you are perfectly cast your friends don't think you are acting at all. They find you exactly the same as you are offstage and they are looking for something more. They don't realize that what you are using of yourself may be exactly what the director wants, and that for an audience it may be enchanting. Your friends only think you are acting when you put apples in your cheeks or snakes in your hair and play Victoria or the Medusa, preferably in drag.

I remember Jane Wyatt talking about working with Frank Capra for the first time in the original film of *Lost Horizon*.

"Wasn't it exciting, working with Capra?" I asked.

"Not particularly," Jane said. "But it was my fault. It took me six weeks into the picture to realize that Capra had hired me because I had exactly the quality that he wanted. That was what he wanted, and all he wanted. I kept waiting for him to direct me, to give me something to act. He didn't want me to act. He just wanted me to be it."

Also actors' friends always have very violent opinions. Not

[171]

necessarily good ones, but strong ones. And very vocal. I called the company together Tuesday afternoon before the invitational preview that night.

"We will have the benefit tonight," I said, "of eleven hundred different opinions from everyone's barber, mother, lover, maiden aunt, and occasional trick: and I just want to tell you now that I don't want to hear about any of them. I know what we've got, and that's what we've got. And that's how we're going to do it."

Don't ever believe in the theater that no news is good news. It is the opposite axiom that I have found to be unfailingly true. In the theater, if anywhere, good news travels very fast, and if your phone is quiet, beware.

During the previews of *The Front Page* the news traveled fast indeed. After the invitational premiere on Tuesday night, I got a call at my hotel before ten o'clock the next morning from Leo Shull, editor of the trade paper *Show Business*. He said he had seen the preview and that he was so excited about the show that he was going to violate the release date on the reviews, which should not have been until the following Monday, and publish a front-page rave review in his paper that Thursday morning. He said he had already written the review and would I like to see a copy. It was an incredible, almost inspired appreciation of the play and everyone in it and everything about it. I read it to the cast that afternoon at the matinee preview. That got us through Wednesday.

Thursday night an actor-friend chased me all over town to report that he had sat behind Mr. and Mrs. John Chapman of the *Daily News* and that as they were leaving the theater a friend of theirs had stopped Mrs. Chapman and asked, "How did you like it?"

"We absolutely loved it," Mrs. Chapman was reported to have said.

Friday night Peggy Cass came to my dressing room. "I thought I'd tell you," she said, "that Walter Kerr is out front tonight."

Jean Kerr and Peggy are great friends—Jean modeled the

leading part in her play *Mary, Mary* after Peggy—and Jean had called to say that she and Walter were seeing the show Friday night and that they would not be talking to Peggy again until after the opening as Walter was very sensitive about those things and didn't want to discuss any play until after the reviews were out.

I was still at Sardi's at one-thirty in the morning when they brought a phone to my table.

"It's me," bellowed Peggy. "I couldn't wait to tell you. I just walked into my house and the phone was ringing and it was Jean Kerr and she said, 'Well, we can't wait to tell you, it's just too wonderful,' and then Walter got on and said, 'You tell that Mr. Kennedy not to change one single thing.' "

We knew Clive Barnes was coming to the Saturday matinee and even in his case, though not so directly, we got a happy indication of how things might be going. The press agent came to me before the opening night performance, absolutely elated, and said that the New York *Times* had called and was sending a reporter and a photographer to the opening night party. I thought this was pleasant enough, but I didn't get excited until he explained to me his own enthusiasm.

"They don't send reporters and photographers to flop parties," he said. "They must have read Clive already."

I am usually a very nervous opening night actor. That opening night I didn't have a nerve in my body. Why should I, I thought. All the critics have already seen it. So I just went out on the stage and had a good time. When I made my final exit in the third act, Bruce Blaine said to me, "I never saw you so relaxed on an opening night. And a Broadway opening at that."

I explained why.

"Did you forget all the TV critics?" he asked.

"Oh, my God," I said. And of course I had. Just as well, if you can manage it. You're always better off not to be too nervous and just go out there and have a good time. The TV notices were marvelous.

Bert Convy had rented a limousine and took me directly

after the curtain to a private little good luck and thank you drink just with himself and his wife at Sardi's, and then the three of us drove on to the opening night party at Gallagher's 33. Everyone seemed really enthusiastic and Helen Hayes and Rose Hecht were positively glowing when a charming man named Sid Zion came over and introduced himself to me and said he was covering the party for the New York *Times.*

"Congratulations," he said.

"I hope so," I said.

"I'm sure," he said. "They didn't send me over here to cover a wake. Besides I overheard something Clive Barnes said."

"What was that?" I asked.

"Clive walked into the *Times* office about five this afternoon and someone asked him what he had covered."

"The revival of *The Front Page,*" Clive said.

"Isn't it kind of dated?" asked the man.

"Yes," said Clive. "Like Mozart."

I relaxed and went about some serious drinking.

The notices, as I have said before, were all marvelous, but not quite that big a surprise because of all the above. But joyous and jubilant just the same. And the play went on for nearly a year, during which time we had in it, at one time or another, more stars than have ever appeared in any other play in New York. In addition to the twelve we started out with, we eventually had, in various combinations, Helen Hayes, Maureen O'Sullivan, Robert Alda, Molly Picon, Paul Ford, John McGiver, Jan Sterling, Dody Goodman, Jesse White, and Butterfly McQueen.

The various personalities were fascinating to deal with. As Jenny, the scrub woman, Doro Merande made her first entrance carrying a broom. It was the considered opinion of the company that she flew to work on it. Doro was always being mixed up with Margaret Hamilton and vice versa. When Doro would walk on in *The Front Page* there would be a universal murmur in the audience identifying her as the Wicked Witch from *The Wizard of Oz.* Wrong. Margaret Hamilton was the

Wicked Witch of *The Wizard of Oz*. Doro was the Wicked Witch of *The Front Page*.

Not that she was really wicked. Just a little weird. She didn't communicate at all with anyone in the company. She didn't like people, period. And considered them unworthy of her notice. I wish that I could say conversely that she was fond of animals, but she liked them even less. She needed all her witchly powers the day she was caught making a slight but subtle kick in the direction of one of Peggy Cass's dogs.

But she was marvelous in the play. It is really difficult to say how good Doro was as an actress because she was such an unusual and offbeat type that when she was right for something no one else could possibly be as good.

I should be grateful to Doro, because it was through her that Bert Convy and I wound up sharing the highly desirable second-floor star dressing room for the run of the play. I had planned of course to give it to the four lady stars to share together. But each of the others came to me separately at one time or another and said they would gladly dress anywhere—Peggy Cass said, "In the eaves, with the pigeons"—rather than share a room with Doro. So I gave all the ladies single dressing rooms on the third floor and Bert and I happily shared the second-floor one.

Our first strange encounter with Doro occurred even before we reached New York. The second Saturday night in Paramus was the beginning of Daylight Saving Time so I called Bruce Blaine and told him to go around to every dressing room and warn the actors to put their clocks forward that night as we had a Sunday night performance the next evening. He went off as instructed and when he came back I said:

"Did you tell everyone?"

"Yes," he said.

"And?" I asked.

"It's fine with everyone except Miss Merande. Miss Merande doesn't believe in Daylight Saving Time."

"What's she going to do about it?" I asked.

"Ignore it," he said. "That's what she always does."

Beginning with the opening night in New York, Doro called the Fire Department during every single performance to report that Bob Ryan and I were smoking backstage. And every performance the Fire Department would dutifully send over a marshal who never caught us because someone always overheard Doro making the call on the backstage phone and would warn Bob and me.

Also, we eventually adopted a phony paging system over the intercom. "Paging Will Steven Armstrong," called out loud and clear on the intercom, meant that the fire marshal had just walked through the stage door and every cigarette in the backstage area was promptly extinguished.

Finally the fire marshal came to Bob and me. "Will you get that woman off our back?" he said sadly. "We don't really care if you smoke or not. And obviously we're never going to catch you. Also, I don't know what she's making such a fuss about. She's rolling her own in the basement."

The basement was a great place for Doro's offstage activities. One evening about the sixth week of the Broadway run, the stage manager called "Places" for the crew and not a single stagehand showed up.

I was near his desk at the time and we were both extremely puzzled. He repeated the call over the loudspeaker and still nothing happened. But as we stood there near his desk we could hear vague rumblings and mumblings coming from the basement. They reminded me somewhat of the offstage sounds of the Arabs in the Jane Cowl show at Amherst. We went down into the basement from which the sounds were coming and found all six stagehands locked inside a great wire cage area in which they usually played gin rummy and poker. The door was a solid one and they were pounding on it with their fists trying to break it open.

"What happened?" I asked.

"We're locked in," they said.

"I can see that. But how did it happen?"

[176]

"She did it."

"Who?"

"Miss Merande."

"She couldn't have," I said.

"We saw her," they said. "She walked up, while we were playing cards, looked at us, closed the door, turned the key in the lock, put the key down inside her dress, and went back upstairs."

I decided that if the key was down Doro's dress it was gone forever. So we got some help and eventually broke down the door and a rather disgruntled group of stagehands ran the show.

"Why did you lock the stagehands in the basement?" Mr. Blaine asked Doro when she came onstage for her entrance.

"It's where they belong," she said. And that was the end of that.

Bob Ryan had the same reservations about Molly Picon coming into *The Front Page* that he originally had about Helen Hayes. But in Molly's case he never changed them.

Actually, considering her training and her penchant for schtick, Molly fit into our production considerably better than I ever thought she would. On the other hand, being up on the stage with her I didn't always know what was going on. When we were rehearsing a scene she had with Bert Convy she asked me if she could sit on the side of the phone table instead of merely standing next to it as Helen Hayes had done.

"I think I can get a laugh," she said. I didn't know how she was going to get a laugh just by sitting on a table, but I said, "Go ahead and try." And I was surprised but pleased in performance when a big laugh did indeed come. After Molly left and I was directing Maureen O'Sullivan in the same scene, I said to Maureen, "Now Molly Picon used to sit on the table here and for some reason it got a laugh. I don't know why."

"I was out front," said Maureen, "and I know exactly why. She was wearing red bloomers."

On the final rehearsal for her opening night following Helen

Hayes, Molly came to me and said, "I have some marvelous business that I do on the curtain call."

"What is that?" I asked.

"I go up with the curtain," she said.

"Up with the curtain?" I asked, really not understanding.

"When the final curtain hits the floor I grab the bottom curtain rod. Then when the curtain goes up again I go sailing up to the grid with it and just dangle there."

I could just see those red bloomers dangling at half-mast over Bob Ryan's outraged head.

"I don't think so," I said, and she never really liked me after that. On a national talk show later on she complained bitterly about the incident and the fact that this "unreasonable director" wouldn't let her do her curtain call.

It is amazing even in a business like ours how little anyone seems to know or realize about himself. Butterfly McQueen, of course, is famous for her unique voice. It is in a register that one would assume only Yma Sumac's dog could hear.

Yet when Butterfly heard that Jan Sterling was leaving the play she came to me and said, "I'd like to play Molly Malloy."

Unfortunately, Bert Convy overheard her and he gave me a look of such genuine terror that I quickly blurted out, which was true:

"I'm sorry, Butterfly, but Dody Goodman is going to play it."

"Dody Goodman?" Butterfly said, aghast. "With that voice?"

LET'S GET THE SHOW ON THE ROAD

I AM NOT a tourist at heart. Not in any way. You could not lure me into visiting any of the wonders of the world unless I had a function there. I don't want to see the Tower of London unless I can be one of the guards. I don't like to be a stranger anywhere.

To me New York is a small town and I am a small town New York boy. I go to the same theatrical restaurants and bars in New York every night of my life and I love them and the people I know there and who know me.

But I love to tour in a play. Why? What is the difference? Well, when you tour in a play you have the best of all possible worlds. You are seeing new sights, new faces, new places. But you are also doing your own thing. And once you have played your first performance you are not a stranger. A thousand people have watched you closely for two and a half hours and many of them by that time feel they know you better than they do their neighbors. By the middle of the week it is rare

[179]

that you go anywhere in that particular town without being stopped on the street by someone who has seen the play or sent over an appreciative drink in the local bar.

In a small resort like Ogunquit, Maine, where I played *Sabrina Fair* two summers ago, by the end of the week when I walked my usual mile and a half to the beach I must have been stopped each day by twenty-five or thirty people who had seen the play and enjoyed it.

There are two kinds of tours: a so-called first-class road tour which is usually in the fall and winter and includes visits to the key cities around the country, and a summer theater tour which is usually concentrated in the lovely resort and vacation areas. The great difference between them, apart from the difference in the locations played, is that on a first-class tour you take everything with you: the actors, the set, the furniture, every single prop, the lights, the stagehands, the costumes. On a summer stock tour only the actors and the costumes travel from one place to another. In the next theater everything else is brand-new. The set, the furniture, the lights, the props are all different in each theater you play.

When I say different, they are indeed different but they are almost exactly duplicated. The doors and windows are all in the same place and are exactly the same dimensions. But they are different doors and windows. The furniture will not be exactly the same but it will be the same height and width. The height is particularly important. If you are trying to act with ease and grace, and especially if you are playing a part where you are supposedly in your own home and sitting on your own sofa, it is unnerving to sit on something you expect to be two feet three inches high and have it turn out to be less than two feet. You don't look very graceful when you sink those extra four or five inches and you are apt to look quite surprised. Before I go into rehearsal in one of my summer stock productions I send to each theater we are going to play what is called a ground plan of the set. This includes specific measurements, heights, and positions of all the doors and windows, which way the doors open, and a firm and arbitrary establishment of the width and depth of the set. If you are doing a ten-week tour you must take into consideration that each of the ten theaters has a different width to its proscenium opening. And you must invariably go with the smallest, as there is no way to compensate for that. And since you have almost no rehearsal time in each new theater, you cannot ask the actors to adapt in that brief time to the difference between a thirty-eight-foot opening, which they have in Flint, Michigan, where we previewed *Bell, Book and Candle* with Lana Turner, and a twenty-seven-foot opening which they have at the Cape Playhouse in Dennis, Massachusetts, where we had the official opening the following week with less than three hours of rehearsal.

It may sound silly, but it would throw off all the timing in the play. In one case it would take perhaps four steps to get from the chair to the sofa; in the other it would take eight or nine. In a light play like *Bell, Book and Candle* every move is timed to exact precision and you could not possibly go through a whole evening playing double or half the distances. So in Flint, they masked their thirty-eight-foot proscenium down to twenty-seven feet, and we played inch for inch the very same movements that we did the following week in Dennis and indeed all the rest of the summer.

In summer stock you play each theater for only one week. Elitch's Gardens in Denver, one of the oldest and loveliest of the lot, is about the only one that has a two-week stand. You usually play Monday through Saturday and travel on Sunday, then have a brief technical rehearsal at the theater on Monday afternoon with the new furniture, the new props, the new lights, and then open on Monday night. I must say, I have a crackerjack advance director named Ron Nash who goes one week ahead of us and supervises the construction of the new set, selects all the furniture and props, and does the preliminary lighting subject to my approval. He stays with us through the rehearsal and the opening night each week and then on the morning following the opening he is off to the next theater.

Organized in this manner, we normally have very smooth opening nights in spite of the brief rehearsal time. Sometimes, however, the schedules are not that simple. Flint, Michigan, unfortunately, has a Tuesday through Sunday schedule, which meant we had to play a matinee and night show in Flint on Saturday, July 2, then another matinee and night performance on Sunday, July 3, and be at the Cape Playhouse in Dennis to open Monday night, the Fourth of July.

This was the most difficult jump of the entire summer and one of the most difficult I have ever made, especially on an opening night. When we agreed to play Flint they told us that they would drive us to Detroit after the Sunday night show and we could catch a midnight plane to Boston. It turned out, of course, that there was no such plane.

So what we had to do was drive to Detroit from Flint at eight o'clock Monday morning, take an eleven-o'clock plane from Detroit to Boston, then transfer to a small commuter airline at Boston to take us on to Cape Cod and a late afternoon rehearsal in a set we had never seen. For all of us it meant getting up at least by six o'clock, and Lana Turner was up hours before that.

The trip was exhausting but mostly without incident until we went to transfer to the commuter airline in Boston. It was, of course, the Fourth of July, and the little plane to the Cape was completely sold out. Lana and I were standing in the window of the airport watching them trying to get all the luggage into the tiny baggage compartment of the plane. It was obvious from the beginning they were never going to be able to do it.

When the flight was called and we started out toward the plane, there sitting on the ramp was the large suitcase containing all of Lana's stage wardrobe for the play. And Pyewacket, the cat, who played a principal role in the play. And my own dog, Poodgie, sitting forlornly in her cage.

Lana stopped dead in her tracks.

"What are they doing out here on the ramp?" she asked.

"There's no room for them," said the Steward. "They'll have to go on a later plane."

"No way," said Lana. And she was Lady de Winter right out of *The Three Musketeers*.

"That's my entire stage wardrobe," she said, indicating the suitcase. "And I have an opening night in just about four hours. The cat is in the play and we can't do it without him. It's Mr. Kennedy's dog and I know Mr. Kennedy well enough to know he's not getting on the plane without the dog. And we certainly can't do the play without Mr. Kennedy. So get them all on."

"There's no room," said the Steward stubbornly. Silly boy not to recognize royalty.

"Make room," said Lady de Winter.

By now the pilot had gotten off the plane to see what all the commotion was about and what was holding up the flight.

"All aboard," he said.

"No way," said Lana. "This plane is not leaving the ground until that cat, that dog, and my stage wardrobe are on it."

Those ladies—the Lanas, the Glorias, the Tallulahs—have a marvelous way of saying things in a tone nobody would ever dream of challenging. I don't know how Lana would have stopped the plane from taking off, but nobody doubted that she would have. She probably would have stood right in front of it on the runway.

But the Captain had no intention of tangling with either Lady de Winter or Lana Turner. He just looked helplessly at the Steward.

"Take off some of the other luggage," said Lana, and I could see some of the other passengers who were eavesdropping turn pale.

"We can't take off other people's luggage, Miss Turner," the Captain said.

"I'm not asking you to do that," said Lana. "Take off our personal things."

By now the baggage compartment had been opened again.

"There," she said, pointing to a huge suitcase. "That's my kitchen stuff. That can come off. That will make room for the dog."

She pointed to two other large suitcases.

"That's my street wardrobe," she said. "Take that off and put my stage clothes on."

She turned to me. "What have you got?" she asked.

"Two big suitcases," I said, pointing to them.

"Take those off," Lana told the Steward, "and put the cat on."

So eventually Lana's stage clothes, the cat, and the dog were all boarded and we took off down the runway with Lana and me looking back rather sadly at our worldly possessions sitting forlornly beside the ramp.

We arrived in Dennis with everything we needed for the play but not even a toothbrush for our personal lives. Our other things did eventually turn up on a much later plane.

The opening night audience had no idea what we had been through. And they shouldn't. That's not their problem. It's our job to do the best performance we can regardless of the problems. And we tried. But it was Lana herself who got that curtain up. And as it went up the cat purred contentedly in her arms, just happy to be there on that stage and not abandoned on a ramp in Boston.

Luggage is a big problem on all these tours, especially for the lady stars. In summer stock, if it is a modern dress play all the actors are required to supply and transport their own wardrobes. If it is a costume play, obviously the costumes are rented. Lana designed personally and had made especially for *Bell, Book and Candle* the four gorgeous outfits she wore in the play. And of course all these lady stars have to carry with them an extensive personal wardrobe for interviews, television appearances, and just because the real stars like Lana and Gloria and Kitty Carlisle want to look the way their public expects them to look.

I remember when Gloria and I were doing *Three Curtains*,

Gloria was traveling with twelve pieces of luggage. She was also traveling with a new maid who wasn't very bright and who was terrified of Gloria.

All the way to Wilmington, where we were opening the tour, Gloria kept saying to the maid, "Just count the luggage. One. Two. Three. Four. Five. Six. Seven. Eight. Nine. Ten. Eleven. Twelve. They're all out in the vestibule. And when this train stops in Wilmington I want to see twelve pieces of luggage on that platform."

The train stopped at Wilmington and Gloria was busy being photographed on the platform and getting the keys to the city. Just as the train started to pull out of the station she pushed the reporters aside and called out to the maid.

"Have you got the luggage?" she asked.

"Yes," said the maid.

"How many?"

"Twelve," said the maid triumphantly. And she counted them out. "One. Two. Three. Four. Five. Six. Seven. Eight. Nine. Ten. Eleven. Twelve."

And she was right. Indeed, there they were on the platform, twelve pieces of luggage. And not one of them Gloria's. As the train chugged by we got a glimpse of frantic passengers scratching at the windows and pointing at their various pieces of luggage which were sitting inexplicably on the Wilmington platform as they wended their way to Baltimore and Washington.

One of the main problems with life on the road is that the local laws and customs are far more tailored to those who lead the nine-to-five life than they are to the kind of schedule a working stage actor has. For instance, in two of the most charming states we play, Maine and New Hampshire, the local liquor laws require a 1 A.M. closing. A 1 A.M. closing is perfectly reasonable for a man who gets through work at five o'clock in the afternoon and has his martini well in hand by five-thirty. But when you are in a play the curtain doesn't come down until eleven o'clock. By the time you take off your makeup and change it is eleven-thirty. And by the time you get where you're going it is midnight. That gives you exactly one hour for supper and a couple of well-earned drinks.

It's really not fair. It's like saying to the man who arrives at the bar at five in the afternoon, "Here's your martini, Mac. Have a ball. And the bar closes at six."

And breakfast. Oh, the pain of getting breakfast in those resorts unless you are up at nine o'clock in the morning, which no self-respecting actor would be caught dead being unless he has insomnia. In these resorts breakfast is a time of day. It happens between 7 and 9 A.M., period.

To me, breakfast is the first meal I have in the day even if I have it at five o'clock in the afternoon, which of course there is no trouble doing in New York. I want bacon and eggs and toast and coffee. Lots of coffee. Try to get it in those resorts. At nine-o'clock breakfast stops. Then nothing happens between nine and eleven-thirty. At eleven-thirty they have lunch. And they mean lunch. Chicken à la king. Poached salmon. Salade à la niçoise. What a way to start the day. Once in a while, if you're lucky, they have a club sandwich on the lunch menu and you can scrounge a piece of bacon out of that. And occasionally a fried egg sandwich. But even if they are both on the menu together, never bacon and eggs. Out of the question. Wrong time of day.

As to the question of dinner or supper after the play at night, there is no such thing. Even in a city like Denver, where I found the most marvelous restaurants during so-called "normal" hours, it was impossible to get anything but a sandwich after the theater. And very lucky to get that. You would think in a city that size there must be some people who work in the evening and who might like to have some food afterward. Apparently not so. They all work nine to five. Then they eat from five to ten and rush home so they won't miss breakfast at seven.

In the resorts even the idea of a sandwich after the show is impossible. Unless you are Kitty Carlisle. All these ladies, as I have explained, can work miracles, and Kitty's special field is in procuring food where none is procurable.

We toured four years in summer stock together and I never ceased to marvel at the way Kitty would con the local restauranteurs into giving us food after the play was over and the restaurant presumably closed.

When we arrived in each new town we would check out all the local restaurants. First, of course, we would find out if any served food after the show. Usually none ever did. We would then pick the most attractive place nearest the theater and that would be our target for the week. We would call up and make a reservation for an early dinner on Monday night. Hopefully by five o'clock, as we both like to be at the theater very early on opening nights. As soon as we would arrive at the restaurant Kitty would ask to meet the owner or the maître d', which was usually the same man. She would explain who she was, as if he didn't know, and she would inquire innocently about the possibility of supper after the play. She would be surprised and dismayed when she found out there was no such possibility. She would explain that it didn't have to be a hot meal, just something cold and delicious. That, too, was out of the question. They had no staff at that hour for that sort of thing.

"Look," Kitty would say, "we have an opening night and we're exhausted and we're going to be very hungry after the play. We're coming in for a drink anyway. Couldn't our waiter just sneak out to the refrigerator and steal us a sliver of chicken and maybe half a tomato and just a little crust of bread?"

She sounded like Number One on the New York *Times'* Christmas list of Hundred Neediest Cases. Who could turn her down? The managers would invariably but still reluctantly give in.

After the performance was over we would arrive resplendent at the restaurant. Kitty would invariably get applause from the bar patrons who had just seen the play. And the manager liked that. She is always generous with autographs and was especially so on these occasions. And the management would like that.

[187]

We would then go to our table and usually on the first night we got exactly what we had asked for. A sliver of chicken you couldn't have pricked your finger with; a tired tomato and a couple of pieces of bread which, if not exactly crusts, were certainly a couple of days old.

Kitty would devour it all ravenously; thank the management exuberantly, invite him to be her guest at the play; then we would leave a substantial tip, sign a few more autographs, and depart on a wave of popularity.

The next night things were quite different. The sliver of chicken had already developed into a full bird, a neat half resting on each of our plates. The tired tomato had mushroomed into a full and gorgeous garden salad. The bread was now banana and date nut. And fresh strawberries had suddenly materialized as a delectable dessert.

The next day was Wednesday, a matinee day, and since there was an afternoon performance that was the time that the various restaurant people usually came to the play. Kitty is the Queen of the matinees. In four years she never played to one that wasn't sold out. The ladies adore her, and although she is always good she has a special glow at these matinees. If she has ever slightly intrigued anyone she will capture them totally at one of these performances.

On Wednesday nights, after we had done the afternoon and evening performances and they had been our guests, it was not unusual to arrive at the restaurant of our choice and find the owner in the kitchen busily and happily preparing a chateaubriand for two. For the rest of the week the restaurant was ours. But then Saturday would come all too soon and after a tearful and well-fed farewell we would have to move on to the next theater and start Operation Starvation all over again.

Since on the road we are all eating together constantly, we have a firm rule that except on very special occasions everything is strictly dutch. This applies even to the lady stars, most especially them, and they like it very much. It gives them a kind of freedom they wouldn't otherwise have. They can suggest going out and ask you to take them, which they could never do if you insisted on being gallant and picking up the check every time. I never leave the theater after a performance without making sure my lady star has been taken care of for the evening. You can't leave these ladies alone in strange towns to shift for themselves. This means that we usually stop somewhere for a couple of drinks, or a sandwich, if we are lucky. And naturally I couldn't afford to pick up the tab every night. Nor would they want me to.

We do it in different ways, all of them fun. Kitty Carlisle and I, who go out for dinner every night, take turns treating each other, she one night and I the next, and we each try to outdo the other.

Gloria Swanson and I do it a different way. We each meticulously pay our own bill. Or rather I pay it in the restaurant and then collect her share down to the penny afterward. I have taught Gloria the strictly dutch and pay-your-own-way routine so thoroughly that when *Variety,* the theatrical trade paper, was still only twenty-five cents she charged me twelve and a half cents for reading her copy.

Lana, Skipp Lynch, Louise Kirtland, our character lady, Taylor Pero, Lana's manager, and I took turns every matinee day taking our little group out to some place really special for a long and leisurely dinner between shows. We took turns picking up the check. And when we said Lana Turner was coming, out went the red carpet. On came the champagne. And it was like Sardi's in its heyday.

Accommodations in summer stock are surprisingly good if you are willing to pay for them, and often you get an amazing bargain. Skipp Lynch and I had an eight-room chalet when we were playing the Lakes Region Playhouse in New Hampshire last summer. It was equipped with a sunken living room, a sun deck, full kitchen, stereo and color TV and we paid $150 a week for it between us. We didn't fare as well the following week when, after a nine-hour drive, we were assigned to the shoddiest motel I have ever been in and which also turned out to be the local whorehouse. We got out of there the first thing in the morning, though from what I observed during a rather sleepless night they did better business than the theater did.

Part of the advance man's job is to secure accommodations according to people's specific requirements. Individual actors have various things that are of prime importance to them. A full kitchen is essential to Lana and she always rented a house. Two bedrooms, two baths, a large living room, and a full kitchen. The extra bedroom was for her personal manager, Taylor Pero, who travels with her. This gave rise last summer to a lurid front-page picture and story in the *National Enquirer* that he was her new lover. Not so. He is a marvelous man and they are dear friends and he is invaluable to her and was invaluable to our production, but it is not a love affair. It is not easy for these ladies on tour and you certainly could not expect Lana to live in a strange house in a strange city without someone close at hand to look out for her.

John Travolta is also very big on the full kitchen and his accommodations have to include his two sisters, who traveled with him and were both in the play.

Kitty Carlisle will live anywhere so long as it has a telephone and Gloria Swanson is interested only in the transportation and arrival of her organic foods.

My favorite accommodations are at Skowhegan, Maine. The theater is actually at Lakewood, an independent compound of charming cottages surrounding a lovely lake with the theater and the restaurant in the middle. Each actor has his own cottage, equipped with a huge woodburning fireplace which can be used at night even in the summertime. There is excellent maid service, the firewood is generously replenished daily, and you can tumble out of bed and walk just a few steps to either the restaurant or the theater.

The Falmouth Playhouse has a charming and very inexpensive actor's lodge with about eight bedrooms upstairs, a large pleasant living room and communal kitchen downstairs, and a special bedroom and bath just off the living room which is automatically reserved for me every time I have played there over the last twenty-five years.

Actors are a gregarious lot and they are inclined to travel not only with husbands and wives but also with lovers, dogs, cats, and parrots. For a long time Tallulah traveled with a lion cub named Winston Churchill.

It was darling as a cub but as it grew older it became pretty menacing, especially to people it sensed Tallulah didn't like. In its later periods it was difficult to decide which was more dangerous, the lion or Tallulah, but the cub was eventually ordered consigned to the Bronx Zoo and Tallulah was allowed to remain at large.

We had four dogs traveling with the cast of *Sabrina Fair*, which included Robert Horton, Sylvia Sidney, Maureen O'Sullivan, Katharine Houghton, and myself. Two of them were Sylvia's prize pugs. One was my Poodgie. And Robert Horton had a giant but very gentle poodle.

If you want to see commandos in action, you should have seen Sylvia, Bob Horton, and myself take over the Detroit Airport when we were mistakenly informed that our four dogs had been put on the plane to Minneapolis instead of to Indianapolis, which is where we were actually going.

Sylvia somehow got onto the communications system. "Ground that Minneapolis plane," she growled in that husky authoritative voice, and traffic on the runways froze. Bob Horton and I had the people in the baggage room lined up against the wall with machine-gun questions.

Maureen, Art Fleming, and Russell Nype were busy trying to persuade them to hold the Indianapolis plane for us but we had no intention of getting on it until we had rescued our four dogs. Someone with some common sense finally opened the baggage compartment of the Indianapolis plane and the four dogs were there, exactly where they were supposed to be. Except they weren't supposed to be, which is what had caused the confusion. They were supposed to have been delivered to us in Detroit so we could walk them before boarding them again for Indianapolis.

Most of our travel is by plane; and indeed that would be the only way one could make a jump to Denver. I cannot remember when last we traveled by train. I don't think you can get to most of the summer theaters by train any more. I have fond memories of one of my last train trips when I rescued Gloria Swanson from one of those booby-trap tiny compartments she had to take when no drawing room was available. The bed comes down out of the wall and when it is down there is no room in the compartment and nothing you can possibly do except sit on it. Well, Gloria sat on it and she is so petite that it immediately went right back into the wall, folding her up with it. She has claustrophobia anyway so you can imagine the ensuing chaos and confusion.

One of the most joyous trips we ever had was during the tour of *Sabrina Fair* when we had to charter a bus from Buffalo to Ottawa, as it was the only possible way to get there. Naturally we had the whole bus to ourselves and the whole cast was aboard: Sylvia, Maureen, Bob Norton and his lovely wife, Katharine Houghton, Russell Nype, Art Fleming, Skipp Lynch, Eileen Burns, and myself. And, of course, the four dogs, all of them jubilant to be out of their kennels and most of whom behaved better than the actors. We had no performance that evening so we all brought bottles of vodka, tons of tomato juice, cold chickens, stuffed eggs, all the makings for martinis, and lots of scotch. The bloody Marys flowed from our departure at 10 A.M. until one in the afternoon; then came the wine with the cold lunches; and at about four-thirty the martinis and the scotch. It was a gorgeous trip scenically; we stopped briefly at the falls; then stopped at six in the evening in a quaint little Canadian town for a very good dinner; and at about eight-thirty in the evening we arrived in Ottawa and floated off the bus and into our beds. A lot of us loved it, especially the dog owners, since our pets weren't confined to ken-

The all-star cast of the 1971 Hollywood production of Light Up the Sky. *Front row, left to right: Martha Scott, Anne Baxter, Don Defore, Kitty Carlisle, Kay Medford. Rear Row: James Doolittle, producer; Michael Goodwin, Russell Nype, Jack Collard, Sam Levene, Andy Girado, and Harold J. Kennedy. (Photo by Wilson Millar)*

Anne Baxter, Harold J. Kennedy, and Kitty Carlisle in the 1971 Hollywood production of Light Up the Sky. *(Photo by Eric Skipsey)*

Poodgie, the author's dog, a gift from Kitty Carlisle. (Photo by Bill Allen)

Don't Frighten the Horses—*Kitty Carlisle, Donna Pearson, and Hayden Rorke. Seated, back to camera, Kitty and Moss Hart's daughter, Cathy, and on floor, Alan Williams.*

Summer 1977 production of Bell, Book and Candle. *From left to right, Skipp Lynch, Lana Turner, and Harold J. Kennedy. (Photo by Chris Kirkland)*

Arlene Francis, Maureen O'Sullivan, and Harold J. Kennedy in Sabrina Fair, *Palm Beach, spring of 1977. (Photo by Carolee Campbell)*

Anita Gillette, John Travolta, and Harold J. Kennedy at the cast party for the summer 1976 production of Bus Stop.

Anita Gillette, John Travolta, and Harold J. Kennedy.

nels in the baggage compartment of a plane. There were a number of votes to do more traveling in that same manner, but Katharine Houghton, who doesn't drink or smoke, kind of put the kibosh on that. She was probably right, too. But it was great fun for a day.

When it is possible on the shorter jumps, I rent a car to go from place to place. As the producer and director of the package I am invariably saddled with the transportation of the million items essential to the show. In *Light Up the Sky* I carried the stuffed parrot. In *Sabrina Fair* the stuffed cockatoo. And in *Bell, Book and Candle* the live cat.

I must say the live cat was less trouble than the two stuffed animals. When I carried the stuffed parrot down the streets of a new city people invariably stopped me and insisted on talking to the parrot. They would become quite irritable when the parrot didn't talk back.

The marvelous thing about renting a car is that you can go directly from door to door. None of that hassle with the luggage and the animals, stuffed or otherwise, at the airport. You can leave when you want to. Stop for lunch or a drink when you want to. And deposit the menagerie right at your own front door.

Actually, the cost of renting a car under these circumstances is not prohibitive. The management is required to reimburse you for what your air fare would have been and if you have someone compatible in the company you can share the car with them, split the driving, and apply both of your reimbursed fares toward the rental costs. So in the long run you aren't too much out of pocket.

I enjoy flying and would fly a great deal more if it weren't for the dog. My dog is too large to be allowed in the cabin of a plane. Not that she's that large. But the airline limitations are such that you can't really get any dog into the cabin unless it is small enough to be carried in a purse, which is what our character lady did with her dog all summer.

My dog has to travel in a special cage in the baggage compartment of the plane, as do Sylvia's pugs and Bob Horton's poodle. The compartments are, of course, pressurized and my dog never seems any worse for the trip. Certainly she would far rather have even an uncomfortable trip than to be left behind.

But I always worry about those instructions they give the passengers as each flight takes off about what to do if the oxygen fails.

"An oxygen mask will drop from over your seat," they say cheerily. "Just pull the mask toward you, place it over your nose, and breathe normally."

Fine. But who the hell pulls the mask forward and puts it over my dog's nose?

The stuffed parrot, of course, had no such problems. But the eastern parrot who traveled with me never had it as good as the western one who traveled with Martha Scott.

We were opening the Los Angeles production of *Light Up the Sky* in Phoenix, Arizona, with a super cast that included Anne Baxter, Kitty Carlisle, Sam Levene, Kay Medford, Don Defore, Russell Nype, myself, and Martha Scott. Martha had been given permission to come to rehearsal in Phoenix two days late, so when they had trouble finding the proper stuffed parrot in Phoenix they called a Hollywood prop shop, ordered a suitable one, and asked Martha Scott to bring it with her on the plane.

She is a lovely lady and agreed to do so. And indeed she did. She walked into rehearsal in Phoenix carrying a moderate-sized hatbox with the stuffed parrot inside it, handed the box to the stage manager and said:

"Here is the parrot."

She then handed him an envelope.

"And here are the two plane tickets."

"Two, Miss Scott?"

"One for me and one for the parrot."

She had bought a first-class plane ticket for the stuffed parrot.

Jack Collard, our wonderful character actor who played a

major role and doubled the offstage voice of the parrot, was incensed.

"If the stuffed parrot is going to ride first class while I travel coach, I insist that you at least give me the damned bird's two complimentary martinis."

Summer stock thirty years ago was an experimental experience. Actors did it for almost no money and they did it usually for the opportunity to play some glorious part, which they were usually wrong for, in some artsy-craftsy play that no sensible commercial manager would ever allow them to do. And it was a great testing ground for new talent. Unskilled apprentices would play monumental roles, usually disastrously, but every now and then a major talent might burst through. It was much more adventurous and in many ways better for the theater.

Summer stock today is better for the audiences, and the audiences demand more from it. There is no experimentation. It is a miniature replica of Broadway itself. The actors get lots of money and they play parts that they are shrewdly and properly cast for. A touring star package in summer stock is as hard to get cast in as a Broadway play. And usually just as well cast. An untried apprentice wouldn't have a chance of getting on a summer stock stage today unless he played the hind legs of one of the horses in *Equus*.

But today as then, regardless of the amounts of money involved, it is still a paid vacation. And it does indeed combine the best of both worlds. You have the lakes, the ocean, the swimming, the boating, the tennis, the clear crisp air all during the summer day, and then a baby Broadway at night. It may well still be Broadway in the cow pasture. But the lights are there. And the play. And the other actors. And above all the audience. And summer stock audiences are the best in the world.

CAST OF CHARACTERS

Mae West came to the Grist Mill Playhouse to do a play she had written for herself called *Come On Up, Ring Twice*. On the sunniest day of the summer she drew up in front of the theater in the longest, blackest limousine I have ever seen. Out of that total blackness a window was lowered and there suddenly appeared the pinkest whitest face in the world. And the blondest hair. That was Mae West.

"How's thuh advance?" she asked me.

I said it wasn't terribly good.

"Yuh got to circus me," she said. "That's thuh only way; yuh got to circus me."

Then she rolled up the window and the car drove off. She looked totally unreal in the afternoon light. Maybe Mae West is one of the wonders of the world that shouldn't be seen by daylight. Maybe she shouldn't be seen at all outside the magical media of stage and film. I got the impression she has somewhat that feeling about herself.

During the week she played for me, we had to hang two parallel sets of black velour drapes directly from the door of her dressing room to the actual door of the set through which she made her entrance onto the stage. This provided a completely private corridor she could walk through without ever having to see another actor or a stagehand. And, what was more important, none of them could see her.

She was good, however, about greeting the public after the performance. But she was definitely granting an audience and neither the Pope nor Buckingham Palace could have done it as well. We had to construct what was virtually a throne, a large high-backed chair with enormous arms, and this was placed on a raised platform which was rolled onto the stage after the final curtain call. There were so many pink lights focused on it that it literally looked as though it were on fire.

When everything was in place the curtain would go up again and there on the throne was Mae, ablaze, and ready to meet her fans. The audience would line up in the aisles and cross the stage single file, getting autographs, shaking hands, genuflecting, or just plain ogling in awe.

I brought up the end of the line on opening night and she recognized me immediately.

"Yuh got a very chic audience; they dig me," she said.

And I never saw her again except on the stage for the rest of the week.

James Cagney wastes not one ounce of energy when the camera isn't rolling. If you were sent to his dressing room to run lines as I was when I was doing a film with him called *Run for Cover* at Paramount, you would find him a listless, lethargic, slightly potbellied, rather small elderly gentleman, sprawled out full-length on a couch and speaking in a voice you would have to hold a glass up to your ear to hear. But don't bury the legend as I mentally almost did. Wait until that camera starts to turn.

When I entered his room only the barest amenities were exchanged and then he said something that sounded like "Let's do it."

He then looked me full in the eye and mumbled something that sounded like "Whychadoit."

"What?" I said.

"That isn't your line," he said. I heard that.

Then he repeated "Whychadoit."

I figured that must be his first line, so I said my first line and that seemed to satisfy him. Then he said something else and this time as soon as his lips stopped moving I said my second line. He gave a kind of nod of approval and then his lips started moving again. I never really heard anything he said but every time his lips stopped moving I said my next line. And somehow miraculously we seemed to finish at the same time.

"Fine," he said, or something like that, but it was a grunt that indicated both approval and dismissal so I departed and went up on the sound stage to wait for rehearsal.

Rehearsal wasn't very much better. I could barely hear a word he said and I thought surely the director or the sound people would tell him to speak up. It seemed to me that there wasn't a microphone in the world that could pick up that sound. But nobody said a word.

My problem was a very difficult one. The scene I was about to do with Cagney was a continuation of a scene I had already filmed on location. It had been shot in the mountains of Silverton, Colorado, and Cagney hadn't been there.

In it, I had jumped off a moving freight car onto a baggage wagon, then jumped off the baggage wagon, and run through the streets of the town shouting that the train had been robbed. As I ran through the streets horses jumped up on their hind legs and whinnied, men came running out of the barber shop, shaving cream still on their faces, and a small crowd of murmuring villagers followed after me. I was supposed to run up the steps onto a small porch and burst through the office door. On the other side of that door six weeks later in a Hollywood interior was to be James Cagney. And now it was six weeks later and there he was.

The scene had gone very well and I had burst through the door at a terrific crescendo of excitement, shouting at the top of my voice. It seemed to me that now that I was picking up the scene on the other side of the door I should be at the same vocal peak. So when we started the rehearsal I was bellowing. And there, coming back at me, was this tiny little voice that I couldn't even hear. I knew there wasn't a microphone invented that could possibly handle both levels of sound and since no one said anything to Mr. Cagney about speaking up I kept expecting them to tell me to tone it down. But nobody said anything to me either.

We did one rehearsal and it seemed obvious to me that Mr. Cagney and I were not in the same movie. This worried me because I knew perfectly well if one of us had to go it wasn't going to be Mr. Cagney. On the other hand, they had all that footage of me up in the mountains and it seemed unlikely that they would want to let me go either. Still no one said a word.

They asked Mr. Cagney if he wanted to rehearse it again and he shook his head no. So we were ready for an actual take.

I stood outside the door in a state of bewilderment. I knew the scene could never play on those two totally different levels. I figured that perhaps I ought to come down closer to Cagney's level. But then I kept remembering all that expensive footage shot up in the mountains—the train, the horses, the horde of extras—and I knew it would have to match up. So I decided that I had better stay as I was and do exactly what I had been doing. It was a fortunate decision.

They said, "Roll 'em," and I burst through the door bellowing. Suddenly a dynamo was unleashed from the other side of the camera. "Why did you do it?" roared Mr. Cagney in a voice that shook the walls of the set. And as he said it he lunged at me, grabbed me by the lapels, lifted me right off the floor, hurled me back against the desk, and we were off.

A second take wasn't necessary and the scene was dynamite. I must say when I finally saw it on the screen it seemed to me that I had a very surprised look on my face. But in Hollywood a surprised look often passes for Academy Award acting.

Anyway I saw the Cagney magic and anyone who thinks it will ever be gone is mistaken. He just doesn't waste it. James Cagney knew how to conserve energy before it became a national problem.

Arlene Francis has a sunny disposition and rarely complains about anything, certainly not about another actor. But she is also a dedicated professional and she knows you can't do it all by yourself up there on that stage. In one of her Broadway plays she was saddled with a young actor who in the general consensus of the company had to be the world's worst.

"He's terrible," Arlene said to the stage manager. "And he's getting worse. We've got to have some extra rehearsals and see if we can't help him."

The stage manager wholeheartedly agreed and they decided they would call a special rehearsal the next day.

That night the stage manager came to Arlene's dressing room.

"He can't rehearse tomorrow," he said. "He has an acting class."

"Well, thank heaven he's taking an acting class," Arlene told him.

"He's not taking one," the stage manager said. "He's teaching one."

Groucho Marx did a play for me at the Grist Mill Playhouse called *Time for Elizabeth* which he had co-authored with Norman Krasna. It had been a flop on Broadway when it was done with Otto Kruger in the leading role and Groucho and Norman Krasna had always felt it might have been a hit if Groucho himself had played it. They were wrong.

The play was much worse off with Groucho in it because the

audience expected something entirely different. It was an inoffensive little play that might at one time have made a mild vehicle for Walter Pidgeon and Greer Garson. With an author's typical devotion to his brainchild, Groucho decided to play the play straight. As a matter of fact, he gave quite a lovely gentle performance. But it wasn't Groucho. And the sold-out opening night audience at Grist Mill wasn't just disappointed, they were incensed. They felt cheated.

As I have said before, you have to give a summer stock audience what it has paid to see. They didn't care that Groucho was giving a lovely performance and playing the play honestly the way it was written. They came to see Groucho Marx as they knew him and they weren't seeing that. Groucho would have been better off doing *Macbeth*. At least the audience would have known what it was in for. And he would have gotten more laughs out of *Macbeth*.

Groucho is not a stupid man and he knew the opening night was a disaster. "Well, I've had my fling with Art," he said, and beginning with the second night's performance more and more of Groucho began to creep into the play. By the Saturday matinee he was pulling a live duck out of the bureau drawer. I never figured out how he found the duck in Andover, New Jersey, but find it he did, and use it he did, and when he left Andover the duck went with him and I am told that by the end of the tour the duck had a bigger part than Groucho did.

I guess I am the only one in the world who never thought Groucho was very funny. He knew it and he confronted me with it one day.

"You don't think I'm funny, do you?" he said to me in some amazement. He caught me off guard and I half-admitted that I didn't.

"Well, you're wrong," he said. "And it's an appalling commentary on your taste. But I find it kind of restful. I don't have to try to be funny with you. And it's like a month in the country."

Even then, back in 1959, he had already become a rather

tired old man, and I think he was genuinely tired of being
funny all the time. It must be wearisome to do a long day's
work, go out for a quiet dinner, and have even the waiters expect you to make them laugh. I'm sure some people like
George Jessel and Milton Berle enjoy it. I would hate it, and as
he grew older I think Groucho did too. But he was a sweet
man and I was very fond of him. And although I never found
him hilariously funny, he did have an amusing style and a way
of phrasing things that was delightful and a little old-world.
For instance, I can remember word for word and intonation for
intonation his saying to me one day, "Would you ask one of
your various nymphs or satyrs to get me a cup of coffee?"

Groucho was a tough man with a dollar. We paid him the
highest salary we had ever paid at the Grist Mill. And when he
went out in the same play the following summer he wanted
more money. And the third year even more.

I finally had to be quite firm with him. "Groucho," I told
him, "if you get any more money you can sell out every theater
you play and they will still lose their shirts."

I thought he would be cross with me but the next day I got a
nice note of thanks and a little check for five hundred dollars
marked "in appreciation." And he never asked for more money.

Sylvia Sidney has become a very strong lady in the theater.
She tells me that I am the one who told her that's how she
should be. And that may very well be true. In any case she is a
far cry today from the shy, reticent, almost apologetic movie
star who came to Amherst College and played *No Time for
Comedy* for me opposite her then husband, Luther Adler.

I say apologetic because she was then very much in awe of
and under the thumb of Luther, and his whole coterie of
Group Theatre actors, all of whom looked down their noses at
Hollywood and anyone connected with it. But she was a movie
star and, as a matter of fact, a major one. She had been in a
number of films which even today rank as motion picture clas-
sics. But she always played the tearful heroine, the pathetic girl

who is drowned by her lover in *An American Tragedy*, the troubled daughter in *Street Scene*, the bewildered and beleaguered fiancée of Spencer Tracy in *Fury*, and she hated that type casting. That was the reason she left Hollywood of her own volition when she was still a top star.

She told me at that time she went to the movies one night to see a picture she wasn't in and they showed a preview of a film she was starring in. As soon as her face came on the screen the man behind her said, "Oh, God, there she is, crying again."

"That did it," said Sylvia.

But whether they knew it or not, and I think they didn't want to know it, Sylvia was a great asset to the Group Theatre. It was thanks solely to the box office magic of her name and Franchot Tone's that the Group got a highly profitable run out of an indifferent Irwin Shaw play called *The Gentle People*. I'm sure all the other ladies in the Group thought they could have played it better. Maybe they could, but they wouldn't have sold a ticket and Sylvia sold plenty.

Her name was always useful in various projects the Group was trying to initiate. But I think the dyed-in-the-wool Group members never really acknowledged how useful it was. Luther told me that they were discussing a project with Billy Rose once and one of the Group members rather cavalierly suggested that Sylvia be dropped from the project.

"Sylvia," said Billy Rose firmly, "is the money ball."

I don't think even Luther realized Sylvia's importance, and certainly he didn't encourage her to realize it. But they made a number of cross-country tours in which he was co-starred and Sylvia was indeed "the money ball."

Those were the days when you played summer stock for almost no money and Theron Bamberger, who ran the tiny but lovely Bucks County Playhouse, told me that he had offered Sylvia and Luther five hundred dollars to do a play for him.

"But that's only two hundred and fifty dollars apiece," protested Luther.

"I didn't have the heart to tell him," said Theron, "that it wasn't two hundred and fifty dollars apiece. It was four hundred for Sylvia and a hundred for him."

But Sylvia was a good wife and a good mother and a loyal member of the Group and she went along with all of it.

Those days are long gone. I don't know what happened in the meantime, but Sylvia is no longer in awe of anybody or under anybody's thumb. She is no longer a big movie star but now she behaves like one. She will sweep into a rehearsal with her two champion pugs, all three of them yapping, and in ten minutes she can intimidate an entire company. I don't know quite how she does it but I've seen her do it and I rather enjoy it. Don't we always enjoy seeing the underdog strike back!

I wanted Peggy Cass to do a play for me on Broadway that Sylvia was going to be in. Peggy hemmed and hawed and said maybe for a while and then finally said no.

"Are you afraid of the play?" I asked her.

"No," said Peggy. "I'm afraid of Sylvia Sidney."

Within the past two years Sylvia has played a number of weeks for me in a revival of *Sabrina Fair* with a variety of co-stars, including Maureen O'Sullivan, Sandra Dee, Robert Horton, Martin Milner, Katharine Houghton, and Russell Nype.

I had no problem with Sylvia, as a director, because I learned long ago to let her follow her own basic acting instincts, which are excellent. As long as she doesn't trample on the other actors. We got along fine when I was also acting in the company. But when I left the cast to rejoin *Bus Stop* I hadn't been back in New York half a day when the frantic phone calls from the rest of the company began. They all complained that Sylvia was trying to redirect the play and was directing them. Maureen O'Sullivan fought with her; Russell Nype fought with her; Sandra Dee hid from her; and the leading man threatened to strangle her, as he claimed she was waiting in the wings to give him acting notes every time he walked on or off the stage. By the time they got to Denver the following week nobody in the company was speaking to her.

But Sylvia is unpredictable. In Denver she decided to be

Florence Nightingale. She tried very hard to organize the company to do a benefit for the Colorado flood victims. The company flatly refused, I'm sure primarily because it was Sylvia's idea. One of the more wicked members suggested that instead of doing a benefit for the Colorado flood victims they should rent Madison Square Garden and do a benefit for the victims of Sylvia Sidney.

But Sylvia has also been unfairly maligned. I did a play which was supposed to open on Broadway, and fortunately never did, which co-starred Sylvia, Barbara Baxley, and Lisa Kirk, produced by Adela Holzer. Four rather formidable ladies. It was the most unpleasant experience of my theatrical life. But Sylvia was a dream and a professional throughout. Her bark, like the yapping of her two pugs, doesn't mean anything. And like the two of them, she also is a champion.

I did a movie called *Macao* with Robert Mitchum and Jane Russell at the old RKO studios in Hollywood and found Mitchum a charming, delightful, and surprisingly thoughtful man. Despite the fact that I had to try to rape her in the film, I never got very close to Miss Russell.

The scene I was in involved only the two stars and myself and it was the opening shot of the picture. I was playing a drunken, lecherous traveling salesman who had paid Jane Russell's fare on a tramp steamer en route to Macao and now wanted to have his wicked way with her.

The camera picked up a long shot of the steamer on the open sea, and the distant sound of wild rhumba music. Then it came closer and closer and the music swelled. Finally it panned through the porthole and directly onto me. I was on my knees, beating out a savage rhumba beat, waving a sash back and forth across my behind and doing something called "shoeing the wild mare." Then a full gigantic closeup of my face, perspiring, panting, heaving, and practically drooling. Then the camera drew away and we saw what I was drooling at. A full closeup of Jane Russell, who was standing across the cabin watching me. I made a lunge at her; she threw her slipper at me, and it sailed through the porthole and hit honest Bob Mitchum who was walking past on deck.

By the time I had forced the struggling Miss Russell backward onto the bunk, the stateroom door opened and there was honest Bob standing there, slipper in hand, and asking, "Which one of you two is Cinderella?"

Of course he came to Miss Russell's rescue; I fought him off; he knocked me out cold on the bunk; they played a love scene over my prostrate form; and when I finally came to, Mitchum squirted a bottle of seltzer water in my face.

When I described that part of the picture where I fought Mitchum off, Vincent Price said to me, "Oh, I see, dear boy; it's a fantasy."

Interestingly enough, Mitchum strongly objected to squirting the seltzer water in my face.

"It's a lousy thing to do to an actor," he said to the director.

"I don't mind," I said. "Actors have had custard pies in their faces for years; I can certainly stand a little seltzer water."

"Well, okay," Bob told the director, "but let's get it in one take. I don't want to do it more than once."

We did it in one take. It went perfectly. Bob squirted me and when I finally shook my sodden head into the camera and they called, "Cut," Bob's dresser came up to me and said, "Bob wanted you to have these." And he handed me a turkish towel and a scotch and water.

Miss Russell was quiet and slightly aloof. Constantly knitting, as I recall. I think for some charity that she is famous for. But she did give me encouragement the one place where I needed it most. I was supposed to grab hold of her by her most famous assets and I was a little reticent about doing so.

"Take hold," she said. "Take hold."

So I did. And if there has ever been any doubt in anybody's mind whether they are one hundred per cent real, they are.

I think the strangest reaction to my appearance in this picture—drunk, disorderly, lecherous, slobbering, hurling Jane

Russell onto a bunk—came from a friend of my mother's who went to see it in our hometown of Holyoke, Massachusetts.

"Harold is just wonderful in *Macao*," she told my mother afterward. "He's so natural. Just the same as he is in your own living room."

When I was doing Shaw's *Pygmalion* with Ruth Chatterton at the Biltmore Theatre in Los Angeles in 1941, Mary Pickford and her husband, Buddy Rogers, gave an opening night party for the cast at Pickfair. Miss Pickford and I were sitting on the steps of the Great Hall, looking down into the room below where Buddy Rogers was strumming the grand piano, playing his favorite song, "My Future Just Passed."

We sat in silence for a few minutes listening to the music. Then suddenly she grabbed my hand.

"Do you know what I'd rather have than all my fame and success and wealth?" she asked, looking down tenderly at Buddy.

"What, Miss Pickford?" I asked, sure that I knew the answer.

"These," she said, pointing to her bosom.

What do you say in a situation like that?

"Bravo, Miss Pickford," was all I could think of as I staggered off for a drink.

A HART'S DELIGHT

I KNEW THREE HARTS: Moss, the King; his brother Bernie, who was the Jack or Jester; and Kitty Carlisle Hart, who was and still is the Queen.

Moss I knew only slightly, mostly socially, but Bernie was the Mayor of Sardi's bar and would arrive there precisely at a quarter of eleven every night and hold court in the corner, puffing his cigar and telling terrible jokes.

After Bernie's death Vincent Sardi had a bronze plaque built into the solid wood of the bar. It read, quite simply, "Bernie Hart schlept here."

Bernie loved to tell deliberately corny jokes and his puns were calculated to make you wince, but he had a sharp wit equal to that of his more famous brother. When asked what he was doing Bernie always explained that he was in town for a series of lower echelon conferences.

I remember one occasion when an actor in John Van Druten's play *The Druid Circle* overslept and missed the matinee performance. One of the other cast members came into Sardi's that night and said with some concern, "Boyd Crawford slept through the matinee of our play."

"Oh," said Bernie, puffing the cigar. "How could they tell?"

Another time, I had been back to Holyoke to be a pallbearer at a relative's funeral. I had never been a pallbearer before and I was telling Bernie about a fact that had fascinated me and that I had never been aware of. This was that after the casket was lowered into the grave all of the pallbearers threw their gloves into the grave after it.

Bernie didn't pay too much attention, as he was on his way to an opening night. I saw him later after the play.

"How was it?" I asked.

"All I can tell you," he said, "is that as I left the theater I threw my gloves on the stage."

Moss loved actors but he was painfully aware of their foibles. As a director they particularly drove him crazy during early dress rehearsals. I remember running into him in Sardi's after the first dress rehearsal of *Light Up the Sky*.

"How did it go?" I asked.

"I have a cast of the most experienced actors in the business: Sam Levene, Audrey Christie, Glenn Anders, Barry Nelson, Virginia Field, and Phyllis Povah," he said. "They all know how to act but not one of them knows how to open a door."

It seems that that night they had had the set for the first time and as might reasonably be expected, since it was a living room in a suite in the Ritz-Carlton in Boston, it had a couple of practical doors in it. The whole evening apparently had developed into a play about doors.

"Moss, how do you open this door?" one of the actresses had wailed.

"You turn the knob," Moss had explained. "You pull the door toward you; then you go through it; then you reach behind you for the knob and close it behind you. Just like in real life."

"Moss, I can't get through this door," one of the male actors had complained.

"I didn't know there was going to be a door here," another actress cried out in frantic irritation.

"How did you think you were going to get on the stage?" Moss said. "Fly on like Peter Pan?"

Of course this always happens to actors on a first dress rehearsal. On the stage itself for the first time in the set, with all of the lines to remember, and the costume changes, and a myriad of props to handle, teacups to balance, martinis to pour, windows to open, doors to shut, it all becomes a nightmare. Two days later it all runs like clockwork, as it did with *Light Up the Sky*.

Moss told me about an experience with Gertrude Lawrence at the first dress rehearsal of *Lady in the Dark*. It was a very elaborate musical play and Gertie had countless costume changes. In his writing Moss had allowed ample time for these changes with scenes that were played by other actors.

At the first dress rehearsal, however, Gertie reappeared on what was supposed to be her next entrance cue, clad only in bra and panties, and sobbing.

"Moss, I told you," she wailed, "I will never be able to make this change."

By the third dress rehearsal, without one single word added to the script, she was fully changed and had finished one round of gin rummy with the stagehands before she had to reappear.

Moss had one quality which I admire greatly in people of his sharp wit. He knew how to make fun of himself. No matter how temperamental any star I have dealt with may have been, if he's able also occasionally to laugh at himself, everything works out fine.

Samuel Taylor in *Sabrina Fair*, which I have played for several hundred performances, has one character make this criticism of the character I play:

"Sometimes it is possible to find the world amusing and not one's self."

How sad that is. The most endearing thing about the late Jack Benny, for instance, was that he always made himself the butt of all his jokes. If you are going to have a wicked sense of humor about the rest of the world, how lovely also to have it about yourself.

Kitty Carlisle I knew before she ever met Moss. I made my professional debut as an actor with her at Amherst College in 1940 in Noël Coward's *Tonight at 8:30* and got my Equity card for that production. Thirty-four years later I did the same plays with Steve Allen and Jayne Meadows. In 1941 Kitty and I did Moss's play *The Man Who Came to Dinner* in Springfield, Massachusetts.

In the early forties I used to see Kitty constantly in New York and even more often on the road when she was headlining in vaudeville or with her nightclub act and I was on my Town Hall lecture tour. We would meet and cling to each other in Detroit, Cleveland, Chicago, and other remote parts of the world.

After her marriage I saw very little of Kitty. There was no breach between us but she had moved into a whole different social world and she stayed pretty much on the East Side while Bernie and I held the fort on the West Side at Sardi's bar. Every now and then Kitty would get nostalgic for her old friends and a group of us, including Ruth Chatterton, Ethel Barrymore Colt, and myself, would be bidden to the Harts' apartment, plied with cocktails and hors d'oeuvres, and talk over old times.

Moss was always enchanting to us but he always referred to us as "Kitty's friends." On one occasion we were invited for cocktails, spent a lovely few hours, and two hours after we departed the apartment was burglarized. Moss told Bernie, "Kitty's friends obviously cased the apartment and came back and ransacked it." He was kidding, of course, but I don't recall that we were ever asked again.

The only regret I ever had over Kitty's marriage to Moss, which was obviously an ideal one, was that it diminished her drive for an acting career of her own. Only Kitty's mother, besides me, ever realized what a potentially first-rate legitimate actress Kitty was, and still is. Kitty's mother was named Hortense but Moss renamed her "Hydrangea," which suited her perfectly. She was the stage mother of all time and terrified most people who had to deal with her. But the minute she sensed that you adored Kitty and were all for her, as she did with me, she was an angel.

At the time Kitty and Moss were married they had just agreed to co-star in *The Man Who Came to Dinner* at the Bucks County Playhouse. Moss had done the play at the same playhouse five years before, playing the Noël Coward part, with George S. Kaufman as Sheridan Whiteside and Harpo Marx in the part that had been written about him. Bernie told me that Hydrangea's last instruction to Moss on the day of the wedding was, "Now remember, Kitty has to have top billing in the play."

In 1970, a long time after Moss's death, I persuaded Kitty to come back to the stage and do four successive summer stock tours for me, the first three years starring in Moss's *Light Up the Sky* and the fourth year starring in a play I wrote especially for her called *Don't Frighten the Horses*. She was excellent in both of them. She is lovelier-looking today than she was in the early forties and her figure is gorgeous. This is particularly surprising, since she is an avid eater. In the three years we did close to six hundred performances of *Light Up the Sky* together and at every one of the six hundred performances she sent the stage manager to my dressing room at the end of the first act to say, "Tell Mr. Kennedy I'm not going on in the second act until he tells me where he is taking me to supper."

It was during the run of *Light Up the Sky* that my little dog, Gristy, named for the Grist Mill Playhouse, and who had been with me for fifteen years, died while we were playing the Cape Playhouse at Dennis.

I have a reputation in some quarters for being a kind of cut-rate Noël Coward. One of my friends, when Noël walked into Sardi's one night, said, "There goes England's Harold J. Kennedy."

But actually I'm a square and a great sentimentalist and a completely monogamous man. "That was it," I said in my grief, "I will never have another dog."

Kitty said nothing, but when we got back to New York she tricked me into what was supposed to be a luncheon date and shanghaied me to the Bide-A-Wee Home where she bought me the saddest, most wistful little beagle, who now, six years later, is the tail-waggingest dog in New York.

In every performance of *Light Up the Sky* Kitty grew in skill and technique as I have rarely seen an actress grow. Even Sam Levene was forced to admit by the end of the tour that she was pretty remarkable.

And that brings us to Sam Levene. Sam Levene is the old curmudgeon of the theater and he likes it that way. He loves to be loathed. He will tell you the most terrible things people have said to him, obviously deservedly, and relish them like a Tony award.

Sam tells with great glee of the waitress in the coffee shop next door to the Huntington Hartford Theatre in Hollywood who had apparently barely put up with him for the four weeks that *Light Up the Sky* was playing there. Sam had had breakfast in the coffee shop every morning with our stage manager, Bruce Blaine. Bruce had to leave a week early to supervise our Florida production and the first day Sam arrived in the coffee shop without him, the waitress asked him, "Where's your friend?"

"He's left," said Sam.

"Well, the wrong one left," said the waitress. "Now will you please move to somebody else's station. I don't want you on mine."

The one thing Kitty and I had agreed on when we decided to revive *Light Up the Sky* was that we were not going to have Sam Levene in it. I had heard terrible tales about him, and even today I have no doubt that they were true and that Sam would revel in them. Kitty told me that when the play was originally done on Broadway with Sam in the cast he had nearly driven Moss into a sanitarium. The part had been written especially for Sam and he was one of the first ones to read the finished script.

Moss invited him down to the farm at Bucks County and Sam was given the script to take up to his room one night. The next morning he appeared at the breakfast table and flung the script down on the table.

"What is it?" he growled, and stomped out to the swimming pool where he sat in silence for the rest of the day.

Sam Levene is not an easy actor to replace and the part had been written for him, so I looked at a great number of people without finding anyone I thought would fill the bill for our production.

One day Sam's agent called me and said, "Why haven't you offered that part to Sam Levene?"

"Because I won't work with him," I said.

"Have you ever worked with him?"

"No, but I know plenty of people who have and they are scarred beyond recognition."

"Do you know him?"

"No, and I don't want to."

"Can't you at least meet him?"

"I suppose I can," I said reluctantly, "but I'm sure it won't do any good."

Sam now does a twenty-minute standup comedy routine describing our first meeting at the St. Moritz Hotel where he has lived forever.

"Here is this man," says Sam, "drinking my scotch, which I am paying for at the bar and which is very expensive. And this man is threatening me:

"'Mr. Levene, there will be just one director on this show and that will be me.'

"'I don't want to direct the play, Mr. Kennedy.'

"'I am told that you always want to direct the play and that you drive the other actors crazy.'

"'Who, me?'

"'Yes, you, Mr. Levene.'

[214]

" 'That isn't true.'

" 'I'm told on good authority that it is.'

" 'Have another scotch, Mr. Kennedy.'

" 'I will. But that doesn't alter anything I am saying. There will be one director on this show and that will be me.' "

It was eventually decided, and the scotch may have helped, that everything I had heard about Mr. Levene was a falsehood. He would do the play. He would take direction like a lamb. He would leave the other actors alone. And everything would be marvelous.

We rehearsed on the roof of the Piccadilly Hotel. And everything was marvelous. For one day.

Then the second day it started. Sam began following the other actors into corners and giving them notes. You don't want actors giving other actors notes under any circumstances, but certainly the second day of rehearsal is too early for notes of any kind from anybody.

When Sam was in the middle of beleaguering somebody I said loudly and firmly:

"That's all. We will now take a ten-minute break. And we will then resume without any nonsense."

Everybody knew what I meant. And Sam knew too. After five minutes of an uneasy silence where everybody stared at the walls, Sam said:

"Mr. Kennedy, I'm ready to start now."

"Well, I'm not," I replied. "I said ten minutes and that's what I meant. Then we will go on and hopefully without any nonsense."

On the dot of ten minutes we started again and everything went beautifully. Sam let the other actors alone and concentrated on his own performance, which I could already see was going to be a gem.

Kitty congratulated me at the end of rehearsal. "I think you've made your point," she said, "and we won't have any more trouble."

Wrong. The next morning it started almost immediately.

The minute an actor left the acting area Sam would follow him with a hundred notes. How to read a line differently. How to walk differently. How to breathe. The actors would try to escape but the room was too small. They all looked helplessly at me. I knew if something wasn't done immediately it could only get worse.

My heart was kind of pounding but my voice was very cool. "Mr. Levene," I said, "we had it clearly understood before you came into the play that I was unprepared and unwilling to deal with all this."

"Would you like me to leave the play?" Sam asked.

"This minute," I said, "unless you are prepared to do as we agreed."

There was a long moment's wait while Sam eyed the door.

I was really torn. I didn't want to lose that performance, but at that point I would have been delighted to lose him. As it turned out, over the next few years I would have been even sadder to lose him than that lovely performance.

"Very well," he said. "I will not open my mouth again."

"Good," I said. And we went on with the rehearsal.

The next few days were efficient but uncomfortable. Kind of an armed truce. But we got a great deal accomplished. And then the change began. I could sense from Sam a kind of reluctant admiration for the way I was directing the play. And he quite unashamedly enjoyed my acting performance. We finished the two weeks of rehearsal in utter peace and quiet but with no particular aura of warmth.

On the opening night in Denver I found on my dressing table a tiny stuffed bear. A koala bear. You turn its behind to the door and it is supposed to bring you luck. Around the bear's neck was a little card.

"Good luck," it said. "And admiration. From Sam Levene."

This was the first of countless opening night gifts I received from Sam during the three summers and two winters that we toured together. Always a little ashtray. A toy animal. A funny, cute, affectionate card.

I remember when we had a dress rehearsal at the Cape Playhouse in Dennis one Sunday night Sam, who drinks very little, thought that Massachusetts was dry on Sundays, so he brought me all the way from New York, especially made at his St. Moritz bar, a chilled shaker of martinis so that I wouldn't have to forgo my usual quotient of two before dinner.

That was the week my dog died. On Wednesday morning, before the sun was up, because I had a matinee that day, I drove alone up the Cape Highway to the outskirts of Boston where there is an animal cemetery which is one of the loveliest spots I have ever seen. I drove there to bury my little dog. When I arrived, there was waiting for me a delicate and exquisite wreath of flowers inscribed "From the company of *Light Up the Sky*." It was indeed from the entire company, but it had all been arranged and organized by that old curmudgeon Sam Levene.

Sam and I worked together over a period of six years in *Light Up the Sky* and later in *Sabrina Fair*. He gave consistently brilliant performances in both of them. He never challenged a piece of direction. He never tried a piece of business, however good he thought it might be, without checking with me. And he was a model of professionalism for the rest of the company.

Very late in the run of *Light Up the Sky*, when we had had many replacements because of the longevity of the engagement, my friend Skipp Lynch was teasing me backstage, kiddingly questioning some piece of direction I had given him.

Sam emerged from his dressing room.

"Mr. Lynch, do you know who you're talking to?"

"Yes, Mr. Levene," said Skipp, rather startled.

"Are you aware of how many performances we have given of this play?"

"About six hundred, Mr. Levene."

"And are you aware of how many juveniles have disappeared during the course of those six hundred performances?"

"Quite a few, Mr. Levene."

"Well, treat Mr. Kennedy with the proper respect or you'll find yourself part of that vanishing race."

In all the four-year period we worked together, with all the presents and with hundreds of performances, Sam never referred to me or addressed me as anything but "Mr. Kennedy." Unlike Ginger Rogers, who did it with a kind of deliberate hostility, with Sam it was a very special expression of an affectionate respect.

"I have never referred to Mr. Abbott as anything but Mr. Abbott," he said, "and I will never refer to you as anything but Mr. Kennedy."

Yet there was a light and teasing side to the relationship, too. One summer, at the end of an especially happy and successful ten-week tour, Sam came to me on closing night and asked whether I would be on my usual stool at Sardi's bar back in New York the following Monday. I said I would be.

"At exactly eleven o'clock," Sam said, "I am coming into the bar. I am going to bend you backwards on the stool, and kiss you full on the lips. And then I am going to leave."

I laughed and forgot all about it. The following Monday at exactly eleven o'clock, with the bar overflowing with tourists, the front door of Sardi's opened. In walked Sam Levene. He crossed to the bar, bent me over backward horizontally across the bar, and placed a firm kiss on my lips. Then he straightened me up, dusted off my shoulders, and walked out the front door without a word.

The tourists were fascinated. Everything they had heard about the theater was true, but they were no more fascinated than the bartender, who had known the austere Sam Levene for years.

"Wasn't that Mr. Levene?" he asked incredulously.

I said that it was.

"Well, I never would have guessed it," he mumbled into his martini mixer.

Another summer when we closed our tour Sam was going directly into the Broadway production of *The Sunshine Boys*. He came to my dressing room and said, "I will want you as my special guest on opening night."

I thanked him but I really didn't expect to hear anything

A *Hart's Delight*

more about it. The play was trying out in Washington and I know only too well how busy and preoccupied we get during an out-of-town tryout. But a week from the opening I had a call from Washington and it was Sam.

"Your opening night seats will be at the box office in your name. I want you there."

So Kitty and I went and were thrilled to see him have one of his greatest successes. No one deserves it more. He is a great talent, which he would be the first to tell you; but he is also a gentle and affectionate man, which he would deny to the death. I hope I haven't ruined his reputation.

As for Kitty, she is now Chairman of the New York State Council of the Arts. New York is lucky. No one is better qualified, as she clearly indicated in less than a year. She is doing a magnificent job. She is happy with it. And all of her chic friends who, I always suspected, disapproved of the idea of the elegant Mrs. Hart ever being just a common, ordinary actress are enchanted. Perhaps I alone am discontented. To me it is possibly one more detour, one more sidetrack from her becoming that baby Bernhardt that Hydrangea and I always fervently believed she could be.

She is so busy in her new job I think it is unlikely she could take time out to act again. Knowing Kitty, I think it is unlikely she would consider the idea of acting when she is holding down such a prestigious position.

If she does decide not to act again, she can press firmly into her scrapbook that last notice she received in Toronto on our final performances there of *Light Up the Sky*. After a three-paragraph rave about her technical skill as an actress and the subtlety and variety of her performance, the Toronto critic wound up his review by writing:

"And she is the loveliest figure ever to grace the O'Keefe stage."

Not bad, Madame Chairman. I wholeheartedly concur. And Hydrangea would have been delighted.

[219]

JOHN WHO?

"Beginnings," Ruth Gordon wrote in one of her books. "Always beginnings."

The beginning of anything is always so glorious, the ending inevitably sad. The final curtain on a play, the final curtain on a life. But even the worst turkey that ever gobbled on Broadway had its own glorious beginnings.

I have written so much in this book about people who are now long gone and others who are in the twilight of their careers. This is a phrase that is very dear to me because I remember Sam Levene chastising me with it when we were playing *Light Up the Sky* at Hyde Park, New York. The theater was a renovated old carriage house and when Sam was assigned to his dressing room he came to me.

"Here I am, Mr. Kennedy," he said to me, "an old Jew in the twilight of my career and you've got me dressing in a stable. And what's worse a stable no respectable horse would be caught dead in."

Anyway, enough of those who are gone, glorious though they were, and enough of twilights. I want to write this last chapter about the beginnings of a new career. It will be a formidable one. It's on its way already and the boy will be a superstar. But no matter how big the name may be on a marquee, and it will be big, the actor's name to me will always be John Who.

He had made a mark before I first worked with him. But not in my medium. I refer rather cavalierly to my medium as the theater. I did fourteen or fifteen films as an actor a number of years ago but nobody would ever remember me, and I'm not sure I want to remember myself. I never did get a chance in any movie to do what it is I do. If you ask me what I do, I would say I am a second man. A second man is a very definite position in the theater and used to be a must when they were writing the high comedies of Philip Barry, Rachel Crothers, Sam Raphaelson, et al. Anyway, a second man always has a marvelous part but it is always the same part. He is the friend of the leading lady. He is never romantic enough to be successfully involved with her. But he is very simpatico. And he always has all the jokes. So if he doesn't get the girl he always gets the audience. And in the last act, when he is sent off into the sunset and the leading lady is in the arms of another man, at least half of the audience wants to go with him.

I've played this same part in a hundred plays. I even wrote a few such plays for myself and played in them with Gloria and June Allyson and Kitty Carlisle. But I never got to play one in Hollywood. I played rapist with Jane Russell and westerns with Joanne Dru and John Ireland. None of these is really my specialty, though I was delighted with a firsthand report Joanne Dru gave me on a western I did with her called *Outlaw Territory*. It was a very strong part and I was very nervous about it. I must have rehearsed it more than any full-length play I have ever done. Anyway, we finally shot my big scene. The next day, when it was to be shown in the rushes, I had an urgent business appointment and couldn't go to see it. I was in the middle of my dinner appointment at Chasen's when a phone was brought to the table. It was Joanne Dru, fresh from the rushes.

"Darling," she said, "your balls rattle so loud you can't hear the sound track."

I've always loved the stage and felt that movies were what Walter Matthau calls "retirement acting."

I had a letter from Walter when I asked him to play Bob Ryan's part in the Los Angeles production of *The Front Page*.

"I'm ashamed," Walter wrote. "I should do it. And I'd like to do it. But I have been lulled into laziness out here doing movies, which is what I call 'retirement acting.'"

But back to John Who?

My friend Skipp Lynch, who has been in the last four or five plays I have directed and who is now practically a partner with me in their production, called me early in the spring of 1976 and said, "You must get hold of John Travolta for summer stock."

"John who?" I asked.

"John Travolta," said Skipp. "He's Barbarino."

"Who the hell is Barbarino?" I asked.

"Barbarino is on a very successful television show called 'Welcome Back, Kotter,'" Skipp said.

"Is he hot?" I asked.

"Very," said Skipp.

I had never heard of him, but I decided to write the name down and ask a few people. Nobody I asked had ever heard of John Travolta either. But, of course, I asked the wrong people. The stage actors who frequent Backstage and Joe Allen's don't know any more about television names than I do.

Skipp doesn't give up easily. He called back a few days later. "What have you done about John Travolta?" he asked.

"Oh," I said, stalling, "he's the one that plays Valentino."

"Not Valentino," said Skipp patiently. "Barbarino."

I sort of wished it had been Valentino. I would have known who we were talking about.

"I've got his agent's number," said Skipp. "Call them right away." And he gave me the number of the William Morris office.

John Who?

I called the William Morris office. "Who do I talk to about John Travolta?" I asked.

"John who?" they said.

We finally got that all straight and they put me in touch with my old friend Ed Robbins, who was the first person I had contacted who knew who John Travolta was. I asked him if John might be interested in doing some summer stock and he said that he really didn't know, that he was handled by a team of personal managers, Bob LeMond and Lois Zetter, and he would have to talk to them and they would talk to John.

The response came back very rapidly. Yes, John Travolta would like to play summer stock. He also knew what play he wanted to do. He wanted to do William Inge's *Bus Stop* and he wanted his two sisters to play two of the leading female parts.

That really chilled my blood. I didn't know whether he could act, let alone his two sisters. I saw them in the beginning sort of as twin albatrosses around my neck. Turned out, happily, that I was wrong.

But I did think *Bus Stop* was a good idea. By then I had seen John on a segment of "Welcome Back, Kotter" and he was perfect casting for Bo. I had done the play before and there was a lovely part for me, which I had had marvelous notices in. And a great part for Skipp. And, above all, the real starring part in the play was that of the girl, Cherie, which Kim Stanley had played in New York. Fortunately that was not one of the parts that John's sisters wanted to play so I figured we could lure a big name into that part and then if no one knew who John was we would still be safe.

We tried a number of ladies for the part. Rita Moreno, who would have been great in it, but wisely decided she was too old for it. Cybill Shepherd, who always swears she is dying to do a play and leads you up to the point where she is about to put pen to paper and then decides to go back to silent movies. Karen Valentine, who had played it the year before in John Kenley's huge theaters out in the Midwest. But anyone who has played for Kenley is lost to the eastern theaters. Because of the vast capacities of his auditoriums he is able to pay television names weekly salaries out of all relation to reality. It is reported that he pays Paul Lynde in excess of $30,000 a week for Paul's annual visit. And that is more than some of the eastern theaters can gross. So Miss Valentine was out. We finally settled on Anita Gillette, who, as in the case of Bert Convy in *The Front Page*, was probably the best casting but hardly a box office bonanza. She might well be one soon, after her smash Broadway performance in Neil Simon's *Chapter Two*. But not then. So we were back to trying to sell the summer theaters John Who?

If I know very little about television names, the summer theater producers know even less. Most of them don't recognize any name since Norma Shearer and Constance Talmadge. This in spite of the fact that television names who have been almost forced upon them by packagers like myself have done their biggest grosses in recent seasons.

The first offer we made of John Travolta to all of the summer managers was a unanimous turndown. John Who was a gentle reaction. In some quarters it was even suggested that I had made up the name. But by now I knew a lot more about John Travolta myself and I was convinced that we had a potential blockbuster.

Mornings as I walked down Broadway to the office I suddenly became aware of Barbarino T-shirts displayed in many windows and photos and posters of Barbarino in every hobby shop. John's managers sent us some clippings of an appearance he had just made at a supermarket outside Chicago. Thirty thousand people had showed up and John had had to change clothes with a local policeman in order to get away intact. As clippings like this began to come in we had them xeroxed and mailed them out to all the managers. We must have sent twenty-four separate mailings before we began to get some bookings.

The first break-through came from Jack Lovett, the producer

at the Pocono Playhouse. He called me up one day and said, "What was the name of that strange boy you were trying to sell me in *Bus Stop?*"

"John Travolta," I said.

"That's it," he said. "I just realized that before the theater opened I had five or six letters from subscribers asking if John Travolta would be appearing at the theater this year. I had no idea who he was. I thought he was an Italian tenor."

So Jack booked him on a healthy hunch. Two days later, Richard Whiting and John Dobbins, who run the Lakes Region Playhouse at Gilford, New Hampshire, phoned me and reported that they had taken a tiny ad in their local newspaper saying, "Would you be interested in seeing Barbarino at the Playhouse?" Not even John's name. Not the name of the play. And they had had over two hundred and fifty phone calls in the first hour that the paper was on the street. So naturally they had to have John Barbarino or whatever his name was and they booked him for their own theater and for the Lakewood Theatre in Skowhegan, Maine, where we ultimately opened on July 5, 1976, and where we broke the seventy-six-year attendance record of the theater.

There is the same undercover grapevine in summer stock that there is in any other business, and other bookings soon materialized. Sidney Gordon, who runs the Falmouth Playhouse on Cape Cod, called and said, "I haven't the faintest idea who he is, but my children tell me they will underwrite the week." And Michael Simone from the Westchester Playhouse, with Westchester's heavy Italian population, was on the phone.

"I have to have this kid," he said. So we booked a total of five weeks, which was all John was available for, as the television show resumed shooting in early August.

Skipp and I both withdrew from the touring production of *Sabrina Fair* with Sylvia Sidney and Maureen O'Sullivan, which was booked for a four-week engagement at the Arlington Park Theatre outside of Chicago in mid June and which would conflict with the opening of *Bus Stop*. We both felt we wanted the experience of new parts and a new play and we were eager to work with this phenomenon we had fostered, at least as far as summer stock was concerned. It all seemed to work out perfectly, as there was just time enough for me to direct the Chicago production of *Sabrina,* fly back to New York overnight, and start rehearsals of *Bus Stop* the next day. As I have said before, beware in the theater when things seem to work out too perfectly. It is never, never that easy.

I was already in Chicago rehearsing *Sabrina Fair* and the first day of rehearsal on *Bus Stop* was less than ten days away when I received a call early one morning from Lois Zetter saying that John would not be able to do *Bus Stop*. He had already signed his contracts but that didn't seem to matter. He had been offered a picture which it was literally impossible for him to turn down. It was a glorious part and a glorious script and was sure to make him a major film star. The director wanted him and John wanted to do it more than he ever had anything else in his life. So it was going to have to be worked out, no matter however. Again, no matter however was not that easy.

I hung up the phone in a state of shock. My first thoughts were, naturally enough, of myself. All those letters. All those memos. All that work promoting someone that no one initially really wanted. Two actors downstairs in the Arlington Park Theatre rehearsing Skipp's and my parts. Six weeks' work we had each given up. And now no jobs to go to. And then I thought of the theaters involved. It would be much worse for them and I couldn't let it happen.

There is an Equity rule, or at least there was at that time, whereby a star can buy out of a contract three weeks prior to the first rehearsal by paying to the management the exact amount of his contractual salary. This has been much complained about by the managers, especially since the incident with John, and it may have been rectified by now. Obviously it is unfair to a management to allow a star to buy out of a play which the management is doing only at the star's request and to leave the management stuck with the entire supporting cast and a play which they would have no thought of doing except for the promise of the star's appearance in it. No one of these theaters had even considered doing *Bus Stop* as a play. It was a personal appearance of television's John Travolta. And now it looked as though they were going to be stuck with the play, and the entire supporting cast, including John's two sisters. And no John Travolta. Obviously unfair. Inequitable. And in the case of Skowhegan, whose opening was less than three weeks away, also illegal.

I have always found it is not wise to discuss legalities with star personalities. Legalities are something they don't understand and don't have to. They hire other people to do that for them. I have also found that the slightest mention of a legality to a lady star drives her instantly to her bed with incurable laryngitis.

These people understand decency, equity, professionalism, and fair play better than they do legality. And it is always wiser to deal with them in that manner.

When I hung up from Lois Zetter I felt that she had represented John fairly and strongly and had really left no door open, but I also sensed that she herself was genuinely disturbed over the situation.

I called her back.

"Lois," I said, "we have no time for screaming or shrieking or threatening or wailing. What can we do to salvage at least part of this situation?"

I asked her when the picture was supposed to start and she said in late July. That gave me real hope. I have never known one of those pictures to start on time, and even if it started in late July we could still salvage Skowhegan and the Pocono Playhouse, which were the first two weeks of the tour. I explained to Lois that in the case of these two theaters, with the short time involved, they would both undoubtedly have to go dark for that week, which would involve enormous expense. I did not say to her that because of the time element John could very probably be held responsible for all the costs and damages of the closings. I am sure she knew that. And I am sure she also knew better than to say that to John. I had not yet met him but I had talked with him very closely for over an hour on the long distance phone and I instinctively felt that he was the kind of boy who would care much more about the damage he might be bringing to other people than he would be disturbed by the threat of his own personal responsibility for it.

"What do you want me to do?" Lois asked.

"I want you to call this boy right away," I said. "Tell him I don't want him to lose the picture, but I want him to stay with the play as long as he can before the picture starts. That would obviously include the first two weeks. And every single day longer that he can stay, even if it is only for a partial week."

She called me back in half an hour.

"John says he's terribly sorry for all the trouble he has caused. And he will stay with the play as long as he can. He will not go back to California until the night before shooting starts."

So we went into rehearsal on that basis. Not ideal. But far better than not doing the play. The dates at Skowhegan and Poconos were definitely rescued. The boys at Gilford, New Hampshire, got justifiably nervous and hired Sid Caesar to replace us for what would have been our third week. This was unfortunate because it turned out that we could have done that one.

On opening night at Skowhegan it was apparent that we had a bonanza. Families came with their teenage children from distances of two hundred miles. When John strode onto the stage halfway through the first act the theater came apart. And yet after the initial hero's reception they settled down quietly and enjoyed the rest of the play. I have always felt it was fortunate that John's entrance came so late, as it gave them a chance to get involved in the plot and with the other actors before he got there.

We had a few problems with the teenagers, mostly when we got into the Westchester area. And yet the problems came out of their lack of theatrical knowledge, not really out of rudeness. By the time we got into the New York area we were having the stage manager give a little lecture over the loudspeaker before the curtain went up. He explained about curtain calls, which obviously the kids knew nothing about. One of our problems was that when John made what was obviously his final exit in the play, the youngsters, not knowing he would be back for a curtain call, and wanting to catch him outside at the stage door for autographs, would rise and leave en masse with still twelve minutes of the play to go. The first time it happened we thought the theater was on fire, and I wished I had paid more attention to Rita Gam's inquiry into what should be done in that case. When it was explained before the play that John would be back for a curtain call but would not come back and would not give any autographs unless everyone stayed in his seat through the final scene, the kids all sat there very attentively and seemed to enjoy it.

From an informal survey we took among the several hundred young people at the stage door every night, we estimated that slightly more than forty per cent of the audience who came to see John had never seen a play before. Asked whether they would be interested in going to a play again, the answer was inevitably yes but only with someone like John in it.

I don't know that there is anything unhealthy about that. Didn't we always go to the new Ina Claire play? And wait for Kit Cornell's new vehicle? And Tallulah's? And who would miss the chance to see the Lunts, if we had not now been deprived of the privilege? I believe in star personalities in the theater. I think it was good that Miss Hepburn came back to Broadway. And Mr. Burton. And Liza Minnelli. And if we can get a few John Travoltas to help us find that new young audience it would be wonderful.

Strangely enough, Anita Gillette had what she called an "identity crisis" co-starring with John in the play. It bothered her deeply that most of the audience was obviously there simply to see John.

"What do you care why they're here?" I asked her. "I agree

with Moss Hart. Have an ass on every seat. How many lovely plays have you and I both done that nobody came to see? I don't care why they're there; I'm just going to do my best to entertain them."

I told her the story about Maggie Sullavan and Robert Preston during the Broadway run of *Janus*. They were co-starred in the play but were not all that compatible. Maggie was the undisputed box office draw and I don't think Bob cared for that and Bob had the unquestionably show-stealing part and I know Maggie didn't care for that. At the end of one of their little "discussions," Bob said:

"Let's leave it this way, Maggie. You keep on bringing them in and I'll keep on entertaining them."

It wasn't as though John's audience didn't appreciate Anita. They adored her and all the rest of us and were vociferous in their approval. Each one of us had a rather effective exit in the last act and the eager young audience applauded the exit of each of the supporting actors as enthusiastically as they did John's. What is more, they were stony quiet when they should be quiet.

I had the most difficult role to play for a teenage audience since I was playing in essence Inge himself and expressing his philosophy of loneliness and frustration. Also, the part had a lovely but dangerous balance between comedy and pathos and in front of an untutored audience it was a thin line to walk. In the second act I had to play a short scene from *Romeo and Juliet*. My character is supposed to be drunk when he is doing this and there are some built-in laughs with the interplay with John. But basically it is a deadly serious scene in which through Shakespeare's lines you see the bitter loneliness of this man and his yearning awareness of a beauty he has never known. I think it is not a compliment to my acting but to John's audience that this scene never once got a laugh in the wrong place. It was an audience eager to learn, and if you showed them the way they followed you every step.

Of course, it was not all nirvana. It is difficult to play Shakespeare to the incessant popping of bubble gum. But as they got more and more caught up with the play even the popping of the gum developed a kind of basic rhythm along with the iambic pentameter.

But Anita had her points and often it was like a three-ring circus, but always a highly successful one. Gabe Kaplan, who plays the title role in John's series, came to see the play at Westchester and came backstage before the performance. It is usual in the theater to come backstage after the performance, not before. Many actors—Anita is one of them, and I must confess I am too—do not like to have people backstage before showtime. I am sure Mr. Kaplan was pressured by the publicity department to come back. In any case, the fact that he was back there before the show was not the problem; the problem was that he was still there when the show was ready to start. And he was supposed to be seeing it from the front. The stage manager sent word to him in John's dressing room that we were ready to start and he sent back word that since John didn't make his entrance for another twenty minutes he would stay and chat with John and then go out front when John was ready to appear. When Anita heard this, she gave a performance of the Medea that Judith Anderson couldn't touch. And she was right, of course. It was enough to cope with John bouncing onto the stage in the middle of the first act, but the thought of Kotter himself clanking down the center aisle of the auditorium midway in the act was unthinkable. A firm word was sent to Mr. Kaplan and he was immediately dispatched to the front of the house, where he caused enough commotion that we still had to hold the curtain another ten minutes.

If John's audience was appreciative of his supporting cast, John himself was more so. He treated Anita in every way as an equal co-star and saw to it that she was included in any appearance he was invited to make. He also brought her out with him when they appeared at the stage door to say hello and thank you to the hundreds of fans who waited every night.

He couldn't have been more wonderful to me as an actor.

He was practically my best audience and if I failed to get my exit hand in the third act he would stare sternly out front like a baleful schoolteacher reprimanding his pupils for not having appreciated Dante or Milton.

He treated me, as a director, with a combination of youthful respect and contemporary warmth. The last time I met him, when we hadn't seen each other for a year, he planted a big hearty kiss full on my lips when we met and another when we parted. I say this with no sense of implication. Quite the contrary. In the theater, long before it became popular everywhere else, we have always been relaxed about an expression of affection. And some of the biggest machos are among the most relaxed and the warmest-hearted.

Now, back to that picture John was supposed to do. He never did it. It haunted us all summer long. It was on again, off again every other day.

Actually, it was always off right from the beginning but John refused to accept that. He doesn't understand the word "no." No real star does. They know what it means when they say it. But not when anyone says it to them.

It was obvious to me very soon after I met John and we started working together and I became familiar with what was going on that the "Welcome Back, Kotter" people were never going to give John the releases he would have needed to do the film. But John never gave up. He was on the phone every minute he wasn't on the stage. He offered them literally a fortune for his release. He would have been in hock for the next couple of years. He was on the phone constantly to the director of the film who also offered the "Kotter" people half of his piece of the film just to get John. But the "Kotter" people said no. John cried on the phone. And the director also cried on the phone. Personally I have never trusted directors who cry on the telephone. I suspect, as Moss Hart says, that they also cry at card tricks. Anyway, it was not to be.

As I got to know John in rehearsal and in the first two weeks of the tour I was able to make a personal pitch for both Falmouth and Westchester, which were still out in limbo as far as the tour was concerned. I pointed out to him what a terrible position they would be in if he never showed up at all and even when he still thought he was doing the picture we worked it out between us and with the theaters for him to play at least a half week in each place. And John was going to pay out of his own pocket the cost of the necessary round trips to California sandwiched in between. The schedule at Westchester was a crazy one. Two shows on Sunday night, a night they were normally dark. Two shows on Monday night, unheard of in summer stock. But they were happy to have the show anyway.

John didn't find out definitely until the day before the opening in Falmouth when he had flown back to California that he could not do the picture. It was then too late to revert to a normal schedule. And the reduced schedules and the on again, off again nature of the show for those two dates did affect business in the last two stands. It was good and the dyed-in-the-wool fans appeared and showed their appreciation but it was not the record-breaking business of the first two weeks of the tour.

John was philosophical about this and about the loss of the picture. For about a week he was very quiet about it and obviously keenly disappointed. Then one day near the end of the week in Falmouth he said to me:

"Harold, you know why I didn't get the picture? Because it was wrong. I was wrong to try to get it. I was being unfair to you. And to *Bus Stop*. And to 'Kotter.' And when things are wrong they don't work out. And they shouldn't."

Whatever disappointment he felt must have been quickly appeased when he got back to California. He was immediately signed by the Robert Stigwood organization to a three-picture million-dollar contract. The first film, *Saturday Night Fever*, has already been released and is an enormous box office hit and John has scored a smashing personal success, including an award from the National Board of Review as "best actor of the year." And an Academy Award nomination.

The second starring vehicle, the film version of *Grease*, is also completed and is in release, and in the third, John will be co-starred with his idol, Lily Tomlin.

I have seen *Saturday Night Fever* twice, once at a special screening to which Lois Zetter invited me and the second time in a regular movie theater with a packed paying audience. It has been a long time since I have heard such an audible reaction to what is obviously a major new movie star personality.

When I was working my way through Yale Drama School a group of us toured in the summertime playing a one-act play in movie theaters as the second half of a double bill along with a feature motion picture. In several theaters we played with a film called *Girls' Dormitory*, starring Ruth Chatterton and Herbert Marshall and introducing Simone Simon.

As we made up in our dressing rooms under the stage for each performance while the picture was on, there would be an enormous commotion in the audience at exactly the same point in the film. The first time we thought there was a disturbance in the theater, but the noise continued at exactly the same point at each showing. Naturally we were curious and eventually we went out and sat in the auditorium to investigate. It turned out to be the first entrance in the picture and the first screen appearance in a five-minute scene of a young actor named Tyrone Power. The instant audience reaction was electric and if ever the audience itself made an actor a star it was true in the case of Tyrone Power. There hasn't been that kind of personal excitement on the screen since then. Until John Travolta.

The difference in John between the time he left me after *Bus Stop* and the time I met him after the completion of *Saturday Night Fever* is enormous. It is perhaps best illustrated by the difference in his behind. That seems an odd thing to say, but it is actually highly indicative.

I used to love to kid John about his behind. When I am fond of actors I enjoy kidding them. Beware if I'm too polite to you. An actor who often works for me once said, "Harold, when you're polite to me it chills my blood."

I had first become aware of John's behind in clippings from

the Midwest describing his personal appearances before thousands of fans in auditoriums, shopping centers, supermarkets, and so on. Invariably mention was made of the fact that the young lady fans would ask John to turn around so they could look at his behind. This fascinated me and seemed something quite new in the annals of idolatry.

"John," I said to him one day after we had gotten to know each other, "I don't understand the mystique of your behind. I don't mean to be rude, but you have what I would describe as a totally utilitarian behind. It looks very comfortable to sit on. But decorative it definitely is not."

"It is kind of chunky," he said. "And you're right. But as George Bernard Shaw once said to someone who booed one of his plays, 'I agree with you, my friend, but who are you and I against so many?'"

We both howled with glee.

But nonetheless when I met John a year later the behind, like everything else, had been trimmed down to superstar status. He had worked out with Sylvester Stallone's trainer. Had taken intensive dance lessons daily for *Saturday Night Fever*. He had worked off a total of twenty-two pounds. All the baby fat was gone. And he was every inch the picture of a young movie star in exactly the old and glorious tradition of Tyrone Power.

I don't know whether the behind is still as comfortable to sit on but it is definitely in the classical mold and could quite handsomely decorate a Grecian urn.

Chunkiness is not for John. In his body, his performances, or his life. Everything is streamlined to perfection. That's why he's on his way to be a superstar if he isn't one already. And a richly deserving one.

Just last year I finished my first summer stock tour directing and playing a featured role opposite Lana Turner in a revival of *Bell, Book and Candle*, the same play I did with Ginger Rogers seventeen years ago.

I had never met Lana Turner before we went into rehearsal.

Naturally I was curious. And eager. And, from some things I had heard, slightly apprehensive. Would she be another joyous experience like Gloria and Tallulah and Maggie Sullavan? Or would the ghost of Louis B. Mayer come along in the luggage? There was only one way to find out.

"Press on, darlings," was Tallulah's favorite phrase. I pressed on.

We had a glorious and joyous and record-breaking summer tour.

Lana had her official opening at the Cape Playhouse at Dennis on Cape Cod where she played to the second highest week's business in the fifty-one-year history of that theater. Our gross was actually only two hundred and eleven dollars under the all-time record racked up the last week in August, the biggest week of their season. The Fourth of July week, which we played, is the poorest week for attendance of the season and we were six thousand dollars over the all-time record for an opening week. Still, if we had known how close it was, Lana and I would have sneaked out, heavily veiled, and bought that two hundred and eleven dollars' worth of seats.

What is she like? More gorgeous than ever, even more so off the stage than on. The figure is a trim, lush 104 pounds. The smile is dazzling, but she saves it for special people. She is shy and almost as private a person as Bob Ryan. She is still slightly insecure about the stage, which is new to her. But she is avid to learn and she is a hard worker. She has never yet challenged a piece of direction I have given her. And she has a sense of humor. In rehearsals I have called her variously Mrs. Fiske, Lillie Langtry, and Dame May Whitty. And she loves it. She refers to me either as David Belasco or Sir Herbert Beerbohm Tree. And lately has settled on George Arliss.

How were the notices? Kevin Kelly of the Boston *Globe* hated it, which is par for the course, and which after all these years I now take as an omen of certain success. Everybody else loved it and one critic on the Cape wrote about Lana as follows:

"Lana Turner is yet a knockout, a gorgeous, glamorous witch! No broomstick. No gnarled knuckles. She has grace and carriage and that touch of class. Her transition from silver screen to theater is complete, and a compliment to her talent. On stage Lana Turner's svelte figure flatters the warm summer evening and her presence rarefies the mystery of the night."

My own notice said: "Harold J. Kennedy, who is also the director of this production, plays the small but important role of Sidney Redlitch and he is a constant delight. One feels instinctively that he is watching a master at work. His performance is like a gift to the audience, a precious jewel to wonder at and to appreciate."

That is a nice beginning and I was going to end with that, but last night at dinner Lana said to me:

"Harold, you have a favorite phrase. 'Never you-know-what with a hit.' This is my hit and I am not leaving it or you for a long, long time."

That seemed like a happy ending for the book.